SpringerBriefs in Law

SpringerBriefs present concise summaries of cutting-edge research and practical applications across a wide spectrum of fields. Featuring compact volumes of 50 to 125 pages, the series covers a range of content from professional to academic. Typical topics might include:

- A timely report of state-of-the art analytical techniques
- A bridge between new research results, as published in journal articles, and a contextual literature review
- A snapshot of a hot or emerging topic
- A presentation of core concepts that students must understand in order to make independent contributions

SpringerBriefs in Law showcase emerging theory, empirical research, and practical application in Law from a global author community.

SpringerBriefs are characterized by fast, global electronic dissemination, standard publishing contracts, standardized manuscript preparation and formatting guidelines, and expedited production schedules.

More information about this series at http://www.springer.com/series/10164

Lokman B. Çetinkaya

Safe Zone

A Response to Large-Scale Refugee Outflows and Human Suffering

Springer

Lokman B. Çetinkaya
Faculty of Law
Fatih Sultan Mehmet Vakıf University
Istanbul
Turkey

ISSN 2192-855X ISSN 2192-8568 (electronic)
SpringerBriefs in Law
ISBN 978-3-319-51996-8 ISBN 978-3-319-51997-5 (eBook)
DOI 10.1007/978-3-319-51997-5

Library of Congress Control Number: 2016963163

Printed on acid-free paper

This Springer imprint is published by Springer Nature
The registered company is Springer International Publishing AG
The registered company address is: Gewerbestrasse 11, 6330 Cham, Switzerland

Foreword

The unilateral establishment and military enforcement of a 'safety zone' or 'safe zone' in another State constitutes a violation of that State's sovereignty, as it is a prohibited intervention or use of force incompatible with the UN Charter and the corresponding customary international law. This will also hold true, if such zone is established for humanitarian reasons. At first glance, without the consent of the target State such conduct would be justified only as either an enforcement measure decided upon by the UN Security Council under Chapter VII UN Charter or a measure of self-defense. Self-defense, however, requires an (imminent) armed attack by the target State or by a non-State organized armed group operating from the target State's territory and the unwillingness or inability of the target State to terminate attacks by the non-State actors against the State relying on self-defense. In the view of these rather strict requirements, which are not necessarily unanimously accepted either, the right of individual or collective self-defense will therefore serve as a legal basis in exceptional situations only. Neither the inability or unwillingness of the target State to terminate the cross-border flow of migrants and refugees nor the fact that the target State's conduct that has contributed to mass migrations into the other State's territory will qualify as armed attacks. Of course, the UN Security Council would have the power to authorize member States to establish and enforce a safety zone in another State's territory. In the view of the current geopolitical situation it is, however, unlikely that the Council's permanent members will agree with, or acquiesce in, a Chapter VII decision to that effect.

Despite the difficulties surrounding the legality or justification of unilaterally established (and militarily enforced) safety zones, a considerable number of governments do not seem to have abandoned plans to make use of them. In particular, the humanitarian situation in Syria and its effects on neighboring States are considered to be so exceptional in nature that the lack of an armed attack or of a UN Security Council authorization would not as such prove an obstacle to the unilateral establishment and enforcement of such zones against the will of the target State. Then, however, the question as to the legal justification arises.

With this book, Lokman B. Çetinkaya departs from the futile approach that is aimed at justifying the establishment and enforcement of 'safety zones' by reference to the *jus ad bellum*. Instead he provides an in-depth analysis of the legality of 'safety zones' with a focus on the law of State Responsibility, but also in light of the highly contested concept of 'humanitarian intervention', in order to establish whether the respective rules and principles could serve as a legal basis. He focuses on the situation in Syria for two reasons. First, the Turkish government continues to consider the unilateral establishment and enforcement of a safety zone in Syrian territory against the will of the Assad government. At least some other governments do seem to sympathize with this idea. Second, and in the view of the dysfunctional UN system of collective security, he provides this analysis because of its practical, political, and legal relevance not only for Turkey but also for the member States of the European Union. Its objective is to provide legally convincing arguments in support of the unilateral establishment and military enforcement by Turkey of a safe zone in Syria that would prevent a further cross-border large-scale migration into Turkey and provide a safe haven for the people driven from their homes by the atrocities of the armed conflict that has been continuing for some years. Naturally, his findings may not be shared by others who are strictly opposed to accepting justifications for a limited use of force other than those explicitly regulated in the UN Charter. Lokman B. Çetinkaya does not ignore the arguments provided by those opposed to the establishment and enforcement of a safety zone but pays due regard to them. He provides arguments based not only on legal writings but also on international jurisprudence and State practice. He discusses the opposing views and only in some instances relies also on rather political arguments. Hence, his book is an important contribution to the current international legal discourse and it may serve as a guideline for political decision-makers.

November 2016

Wolff Heintschel von Heinegg
Europa-Universität Viadrina, Frankfurt (Oder), Germany

Contents

Chapter 1
Introduction

A safe zone can be defined as demarcated place protected by foreign military forces to ensure security of people who flee danger within their own country. If successfully established and maintained such zones eliminate security concerns of displaced persons, refugees, and at-risk civilians and aim to keep those groups within their own country. This function of safe zones gives refugee-receiving States an appropriate means to prevent persons from seeking refuge by crossing an international border.

There is not a consistent term in the international legal literature for such zones. The diversity and interchangeability of phrases—including 'safe havens,' 'safe zones,' 'safe areas,' 'security zones,' 'safety zones,' 'neutralized zones,' and 'protected areas'—creates ambiguity.[1] In order not to give rise to such ambiguity, only the concept of 'safe zone' is used in this paper. In addition, the term 'refugee' is used and defined as persons who flee danger across international borders to seek safety, regardless of which status is given to them by receiving States.

As it is unlikely to consider a large-scale refugee influx itself triggering an armed conflict between refugee-receiving and refugee-generating States, as is the case between Turkey and Syria, the establishment of a safe zone needs to be justified, if at all possible, under *jus ad bellum*. Therefore, the concept of safe zone[s] as used in this paper is different from the similar concepts regulated under international humanitarian law (IHL). Furthermore, while IHL zones can only be created with the consent of parties to the conflict, it is discussed here whether a safe zone can be established by outside powers in time of peace.

As the expression 'large-scale' indicates, legality of safe zones is discussed in this paper only when a State facing an overwhelming flow of refugees across international borders. Therefore the establishment of a safe zone is not a measure applicable to every refugee outflow situation. A refugee influx cannot be categorized as

[1] Jean-Philippe Lavoyer, 'International Humanitarian Law, Protected Zones and the Use of Force', in W. Biermann & M. Vadset (eds) *UN Peacekeeping in Trouble: Lessons Learned from the Former Yugoslavia* (Brookfield: Ashgate, 1998) 262, at 262.

L.B. Çetinkaya, *Safe Zone*, SpringerBriefs in Law,
DOI 10.1007/978-3-319-51997-5_1

large-scale by merely looking at number of persons, though it is one of the major indicators. Instead, as each refugee situation is unique, it should be evaluated on a case-by-case basis taking into consideration the special circumstances of each situation.

History continues to show that an outbreak of armed hostilities accompanied by gross and systematic human rights violations often compels persons to flee their homeland. In turn, those people who flee such danger begin knocking on their neighboring State's door. Then that State must decide whether to leave these people to die or embrace them at a cost to the wellbeing of its own citizens.[2]

States which face a large-scale refugee influx have strong interests in keeping displaced populations in their country of origin and enabling refugees to return home. This is due to the fact that such an influx may affect the economic, political, and social stability, as well as the maintenance of the order and security of the community, of the receiving State, and also carry adverse consequences for inter-State relations, thus endangering international peace and security. For instance, Syria does not pose a direct security threat to its neighbors, but its instability and large-scale outflows of refugees emanating from its territory have had destabilizing consequences in the region. This internationalizes what might otherwise be purely an internal issue. Therefore it is significant for States to take action aimed at preventing those displaced populations from becoming refugees by keeping them in their own country. In this sense, the establishment of safe zones appears to be an appropriate measure to ensure security to persons who flee conflict and violence within their own country so that they do not become refugees. Additionally, those zones may play an important role to avert human suffering in today's world of internal warfare.

It must be clearly stressed from the beginning that the aim of a safe zone is to avert a large-scale outflow of refugees by ensuring security to those who flee human suffering until such fear does not exist anymore. This work argues that safe zones can be an effective way to achieve the dual purpose of humanitarian protection and safeguarding of the interests of refugee-receiving States. Furthermore, the establishment of safe zone does not constitute an undue intervention into the internal affairs of the target State while it internationalizes its internal affairs by initiating and failing to prevent large-scale outflows of its people that threatens other States' interests as well as regional peace and security.

The underlying reason of the difficulty in the determination of a lawful response to a large-scale movement of population across international borders is that it has more recently become a more frequent problem of inter-State relations. Therefore customary international law has no apparent specific rule on this issue. However, it requires interpretation and adaptation of the existing rules and principles of international law in addition to State practices and jurisprudence of international courts in finding possible appropriate lawful responses to such situations. This work

---

[2]Stanley Hoffman, *Duties beyond Borders: On the Limits and Possibilities of Ethical International Politics* (New York: Syracuse University Press, 1981), at 111.

attempts to survey whether the establishment of safe zones, under certain circumstances, would be permissible under international law in order for a refugee-receiving State to preserve its interests by averting and even reversing such flows by ensuring safety of refugees, displaced persons and at-risk civilians within their national homeland.

This book attempts to survey possible justifications for the establishment of safe zones in countries within which a large-scale refugee outflow is generated by advancing legal arguments consistent with international law. The intention of this survey should not be misinterpreted as seeking a way to undermine the limits of the general prohibition on the use or threat of force by broadening its exceptions. Instead, the book addresses State practice to demonstrate whether other possible exceptional circumstances in customary international law can be relied upon to establish a safe zone.

According to the predominant view, all uses of force are prohibited under *jus ad bellum* regime, save for the two codified exceptions in the UN Charter which are self-defense, recognized in Article 51, and forcible measures that are adopted or authorized by the Security Council under Chapter VII. In addition, a State may consent to military operations by foreign forces on its territory.[3] However, as none of these exceptions seem available to refugee-receiving State[s] to deal with the unwanted large-scale influx of Syrian refugees, the book surveys whether establishment of safe zone may be justified by following arguments.

First, this work argues that the prohibition on the use of force does not apply to countermeasures, addressed under Chap. 2, if we accept the gap between armed attack and use of force. Therefore, if establishment of safe zone is a proportionate measure according to the existing conditions of a case, then it may be justified on the ground of countermeasures. Furthermore, under exceptional circumstances, limited military actions on the territory of a refugee-generating State to establish and maintain a safe zone with the aim of reducing refugee outflows by eliminating the need for flight, may also be justified by a state of necessity, addressed under Chap. 3. Moreover, the book explores whether and under what circumstances outside intervention by the establishment of safe zones may be justified under the concept of humanitarian intervention, addressed under Chap. 4.

The suitability of safe zones as a response to overwhelming influx of individuals across international borders depends on the conditions that generate, or carry the potential to generate, outflows. Since the proposal of safe zone for Syria continues to remain on the international community's agenda, the specific conditions of this case are particularly addressed in order to analyze the suitability and legality of a possible safe zone in Syria.

[3]See, e.g., *Military and Paramilitary Activities in and against Nicaragua (Nicaragua v US)*, ICJ Reports 1986, 14, para 246.

Chapter 2
Application of Countermeasures to Justify the Establishment of Safe Zones as a Response to Large-Scale Refugee Outflows

Article 13(1)(a) of the UN Charter includes 'encouraging the progressive development of international law and its codification' as one of the purposes for which the UN General Assembly is empowered to 'initiate studies and make recommendations.' The International Law Commission (ILC) was created by the General Assembly in 1947 in order to meet this expectation. Therefore, the ILC's Draft Articles on Responsibility of States for Internationally Wrongful Acts (ARSIWA) can be seen as an attempt to contribute to the progressive development of international law.[1] However, one must be aware that Articles 22, 49–54 ARSIWA, dedicated to countermeasures, do not entirely reflect customary law. Formulation of countermeasures under ARSIWA may be somewhat idealistic with the aim to prevent any escalation of the situation.

As there is no provision in any convention that regulates countermeasures under international law, it is questionable as to whether a State is even allowed to use countermeasures in response to its 'belief' that an internationally wrongful act has been perpetrated by another State. Alland addresses this, stating that, 'it is a mechanism of general international law which exists implicitly and independently of any particular provision.'[2] Judicial decisions, State practice, and the international law doctrine clearly reveal that States are permitted to take countermeasures meeting certain substantive and procedural conditions in response to a previous internationally wrongful act of another State directed against itself.[3] However, there is not yet a consensus on the substantive conditions of the countermeasures.

---

[1]Articles on the Responsibility of States for Internationally Wrongful Acts, II(2) *Yearbook of the International Law Commission* 26 (2001), (*ARSIWA*).
[2]Denis Alland, 'The Definition of Countermeasures', in: J. Crawford, A. Pellet & S. Olleson (eds) *The Law of International Responsibility* (New York: OUP, 2010) 1127, at 1129.
[3]Commentary to the Articles on the Responsibility of States for Internationally Wrongful Acts, II (2) *Yearbook of the International Law Commission* 36 (2001), Art 22, para 2 (*ARSIWA Commentary*).

L.B. Çetinkaya, *Safe Zone*, SpringerBriefs in Law,
DOI 10.1007/978-3-319-51997-5_2

2.1 Analysis of the Requirements for a Countermeasures Defense to Establish of Safe Zones

The establishment of safe zones by a refugee-receiving State may be considered a countermeasure against a refugee-generating State provided that and for so long as the necessary conditions for taking countermeasures are satisfied. However, countermeasures would still be liable to abuse and misuse, as the criteria for a State to unilaterally adopt countermeasures remains uncertain. For instance, safe zones may be created with the aim of paving the way for annexation in future, or to strengthen the impact of a State over the dispute. In order to prevent such abuses in the name of countermeasures and to keep it within generally accepted bounds, it is vital to address in detail the conditions, limitations and their requirements set out in State practice.

2.1.1 A Response to a Previous Internationally Wrongful Act

As has been indicated by the International Court of Justice (ICJ) in the case concerning *Gabčíkovo–Nagymaros Project*,[4] only a prior violation of an international law obligation may entitle the injured State to adopt countermeasures against a State responsible for that internationally wrongful act. When a State's act constitutes a breach of an international obligation, that act is considered an internationally wrongful act.

It is true that the injured State makes its own assessment regarding the existence of an internationally wrongful act, but any unjustified belief by the injured State on its existence would not be sufficient to adopt countermeasures against the other State. Therefore, although determination of the existence of an internationally wrongful act is at the discretion of injured State[s], it is still expected for such a belief to be justified regarding the existence of an internationally wrongful act.

Initiating a large-scale refugee movement into the territory of another State against the will of that State qualifies as a violation of its sovereignty, specifically the sovereign right to determine who is allowed to enter its territory. Moreover, to control access to and egress from its territory is not only a right but also an obligation of due diligence that is owed by one State to another by virtue of territorial sovereignty.[5] The State that does not forestall such movements from its territory to another country is violating its positive obligation of due diligence

[4] *Gabčíkovo-Nagymaros Project (Hungary v Slovakia),* ICJ Reports 1997, 7, para 83.

[5] Sarah Heathcote, 'State Omissions and Due Diligence: Aspects of Fault, Damage and Contribution to Injury in the Law of State Responsibility', in: K. Bannelier, T. Christakis, S. Heathcote (eds) *The ICJ and the Evolution of International Law: The Enduring Impact of the Corfu Channel Case* (UK: Routledge, 2012) 295, at 299.

recognized as one of the principles of responsibility in international law, widely referred as a 'basic principle of international law.'[6] For example, Syria's continuing failure to halt the large-scale outflow of refugees across international borders demonstrates a breach of its due diligence obligation to protect other States' rights in its own territory. Thus, Syria bears responsibility for its failure to act with due diligence in the context of large-scale refugee outflow to Turkey.

The question in the Syrian case is as follows: does the omission—indeed, the complete failure—of the Assad government to carry out its duties to take appropriate preventive measures, in full knowledge of the situation, entitle Turkey on its own initiative to act in its stead? This question was raised when the Royal Navy decided to carry out minesweeping operations (*Operation Retail*) without Albania's consent in its waters of the *Corfu Channel*. The ICJ in that case ruled that States are obliged not to allow knowingly its territory to be used for acts contrary to the rights of other States.[7] Previously, the tribunal in the *Trail Smelter* arbitration, maybe for the first time in international law,[8] stated the principle that '[a] [S]tate owes at all times a duty to protect other [S]tates against injurious acts by individuals from within its jurisdiction.'[9] According to Jennings, Oppenheim and subsequent scholars,[10] the source of this obligation can be found in the generally accepted doctrine of the abuse of rights, which is referred in common law as *sic utere tuo ut alienum non laedas* ('use your own property in such a manner as not to injure that of another') that is also applicable in international law as a general principle within the meaning of Article 38(1)(c) of the ICJ Statute. Hence, if a State has the knowledge of large-scale refugee influx toward international borders originating from its territory and liable to violate other States' rights, its failure for taking appropriate acts to protect the interests of other States faced with such influx may trigger the due diligence obligation of the refugee-generating State.

The large-scale refugee outflow from Syria to Turkey can lead to international responsibility for Syria because of the lack of due diligence on the part of the Syrian authorities to forestall these movements. One should not narrow the scope of this obligation to criminal acts[11]; rather it applies to all activities inflicting—or having

---

[6]See, *inter alia*, Robert P. Barnidge, Jr. 'The Due Diligence Principle Under International Law', 8 *International Community Law Review* 81 (2006), at 121; Luigi Condorelli, 'The Imputability to States of Acts of International Terrorism', 19 *Israel Yearbook on Human Rights* 233 (1989), at 241.

[7]*Corfu Channel (United Kingdom v Albania), ICJ Reports 1949, 1*, at 22.

[8]Antonio Cassese, *International Law* (2nd edn, OUP, 2010) at 484.

[9]*Trail Smelter Arbitration (United States v. Canada),* 35 *American Journal of International Law* 684 (1941), at 713.

[10]Robert Y. Jennings, 'Some International Law Aspects of the Refugee Question', 20 *British Yearbook of International Law* 98 (1939), at 112; Lassa Oppenheim, *International Law,* Vol. 1: Peace, H. Lauterpacht, (ed) (8th edn, London: Longmans, Green, 1955), at 346–347; Ian Brownlie, *Principles of Public International Law* (3rd edn, UK: OUP, 1979), at 443–445.

[11]Michael N. Schmitt, 'Preemptive Strategies in International Law', 24 *Michigan Journal of International Law* 513 (2003), at 540 *et seq.*

the potential of inflicting—severe damage to the rights of the target State.[12] The complete failure of the Syrian government to prevent large-scale refugee outflow inflicts severe damage to the security and the social, political, and economic stability of Turkey. Syria must therefore suffer the consequence of having Turkey, if decides to do so, establish safe zones within Syria. In other words, if Syria has not had the means at its disposal to perform its obligations to prevent trans-border security threats originating from its territory, then it must allow Turkey to do so.

Were Syria to demonstrate that it had taken all appropriate steps to halt the outflow of refugees in this situation, it would not be responsible for a breach. This is because, as Dupuy indicates,[13] the due diligence obligation requires the State's 'best effort.' As Barnidge rightly indicates,[14] this obligation requires undertaking all possible measures that could be reasonably expected from a State to protect other States' rights in its own territory. However, without such efforts, it definitely qualifies as a breach of the due diligence obligation. Hence, had the Assad government shown a willingness and capability to take appropriate measures to control its border, it could be argued that there is no justification for Turkey to resort to such countermeasures. However, the unwillingness and complete failure of the Assad regime to take prompt and efficient action in response to large-scale refugee outflow from its territory to Turkey gives rise to Syria's international responsibility within the context of large-scale refugee outflow to Turkey.

As Goodwin-Gill rightly concludes,[15] by relying on the established rules of international law, States are bound by a general principle not to allow large-scale movements of people across national borders and to co-operate with other States in the resolution of such problems. If a State fails to take appropriate preventive measures in order to protect the interests of other States, then it must suffer the consequence of having the other State take countermeasures on its territory.

2.1.2 The Responsible State Must Be Called upon to Return to a Lawful Situation Before Countermeasures Are Adopted

The injured State is first required to call upon the responsible State to return to a lawful situation before taking countermeasures according to the general practice of

[12]Wolff Heintschel von Heinegg, 'Legal Implications of Territorial Sovereignty in Cyberspace', in: C. Czosseck, R. Ottis & K. Ziolkowski (eds), *4th International Conference on Cyber Conflict* (Tallinn: NATO CCD COE Publications, 2012) 7, at 16.

[13]Pierre-Marie Dupuy, 'Reviewing the Difficulties of Codification: On Ago's Classification of Obligations of Means and Obligations of Result in Relation to State Responsibility', 10(2) *European Journal of International Law* 371 (1999), at 378.

[14]Robert P. Barnidge, Jr, *supra* note 6, at 117.

[15]Guy S. Goodwin-Gill, *The Refugee in International Law* (UK:OUP, 1983) at 228.

States[16] as has been indicated by the ICJ in the case concerning *Gabčíkovo–Nagymaros Project*,[17] and by the tribunals in the cases of *Air Service Agreement*[18] and *Naulilaa*.[19] After the first condition has failed, Article 52(1)(b) ARSIWA requires the injured State to notify the responsible State of its decision to take countermeasures and to offer to negotiate with that State.[20] This second condition offers another way out to the responsible State, allowing it to reconsider its position and offering the possibility of reaching a peaceful settlement. However, this obligation does not have a basis in customary international law. The position of ARSIWA, therefore, seems somewhat idealistic, but to consider it the other way would be to open the door to escalation of conflicts through counter-countermeasures.

If Turkey decides to adopt the countermeasure of establishing safe zones, it must first call upon Syria to halt the large-scale outflow of refugees from its territory to Turkey. However, the consent of the State in whose territory such a zone is to be established would not be deemed a pre-condition in the case that the State continuously fails to comply with its international obligation of protecting other States' rights within its territory.[21] Therefore if the Syrian government still fails to take appropriate measures to attempt to prevent such movements, only then would Turkey be justified in establishing safe zones in Syria.

2.1.3 Countermeasures Must Be Directed Only Against the Wrongdoer State to Induce Compliance with Its International Obligations

As has been indicated by the ICJ in the case concerning *Gabčíkovo–Nagymaros Project*,[22] countermeasures must be directed only against the State which is the author of that internationally wrongful act, not against third parties. As the phrases 'if and to the extent' and 'countermeasures taken against' emphasize in Article 22 ARSIWA, countermeasures may only be justified in relations between an injured State and the State which has committed the internationally wrongful act.

Inducing the responsible State to comply with its international obligations is the limited object and exceptional nature of countermeasures as has been indicated by

[16] ARSIWA Art 52 (1)(a); ARSIWA Commentary, Art 52, para 3.

[17] *Gabčíkovo-Nagymaros Project (Hungary v Slovakia)*, ICJ Reports 1997, 7, para 84.

[18] *Air Service Agreement of 27 March 1946* (US v. France), 18 *RIAA* 416 (1978), paras 85-87.

[19] *Naulilaa Incident* (Portugal v Germany) 2 RIAA 1011 (1928), at 1026.

[20] ARSIWA Art 52(1)(b).

[21] B. S. Chimni, 'The Incarceration of Victims: Deconstructing Safety Zones', in: N. Al-Nauimi & R. Meese (eds), *International Legal Issues Arising Under the United Nations Decade of International Law* (The Netherlands: Martinus Nijhoff Publishers, 1995) 823, at 827.

[22] *Gabčíkovo-Nagymaros Project (Hungary v Slovakia)*, ICJ Reports 1997, 7, para 83.

the use of word "only" in article 49(1) ARSIWA. Therefore, countermeasures must be considered an instrument for achieving the restoration of a condition of legality between injured and responsible States, not as a form of punishment.[23] This is not retaliation, but rather inducing the wrongdoer to terminate its internationally wrongful act, to return to lawful conduct, and to comply with its international obligations.

As Syria has been violating both its obligation of due diligence and the sovereignty of neighboring States, Turkey may take the countermeasure of establishing safe zones to procure the cessation of a continuing influx of refugees unless Syria demonstrates willingness and capability to comply with its international obligation of protecting the interests of its neighboring countries by adopting measures to terminate that outflow.

2.1.4 Duration

According to Article 49(2) ARSIWA, the inherent temporal limitation of countermeasures is that the injured State is allowed to sustain its adopted countermeasures as long as the responsible State maintained the non-performance of its own international obligations, i.e., the failure of the Assad government to exercise due diligence over its borders within the context of large-scale refugee outflow.

Article 53 ARSIWA requires the injured State to cease its countermeasures as soon as the responsible State returns to the lawful situation. In a similar manner, Article 52(3) ARSIWA requires the injured State not to take countermeasures, or to suspend without undue delay, if that State has already met the following circumstances. First, if the responsible State terminates its internationally wrongful act, then the reason for the countermeasures disappears. Second, if the dispute appears before an authorized court or tribunal whose decisions are binding on the parties, then that court or tribunal, if it deems necessary, may order adoption of certain countermeasures as an interim measure. This is because the mandatory character of provisional measures has been recognized since the *LaGrand* case.[24] Consequently, the injured State would be deprived of justification if it maintains its countermeasures from the moment when one of these circumstances occurs. However, countermeasures may also be effectively reactivated when the conditions for the suspension or termination disappear.

As long as the Assad government refuses to put an end to its continuous injurious act that violates Turkey's sovereign right to determine who is allowed to enter its territory, Turkey may lawfully establish a safe zone in Syria that would be justified under countermeasures. Determination of the length of time for which it is established depends on and must be limited to the needs of the situation that

---

[23]ARSIWA Commentary, Art 49, para 7.

[24]*LaGrand (Germany v USA)*, ICJ Reports 2001, 466, para 103.

triggered these countermeasures.[25] Should the Syrian government become able and willing to ensure the safety of persons in Syria, thereby halting the outflow and perhaps even triggering the return of previously displaced persons, the need for such countermeasures would disappear. In addition, if Syria were to exercise due diligence over its borders by effectively averting the outflow of refugees, the conditions legitimizing the adoption of such countermeasures would disappear instantly. However, in the latter case, if Turkey returns Syrian refugees who have been hosted in its country to the imminent risk of persecution before the situation that triggered their outflow has sufficiently improved, then Turkey would be violating its *non-refoulement* obligation which is of customary character[26] and enshrined in many instruments such as Article 33(1) 1951 Refugee Convention,[27] Article 3(1) Convention Against Torture[28] and Article II (3) OAU Convention Governing the Specific Aspects of Refugee Problems in Africa.[29]

2.1.5 Reversibility

Although the ICJ obliged States to select countermeasures which are reversible in their effects,[30] the ILC did not articulate this as an absolute duty. It used instead the expression 'as far as possible' in Article 49(3) ARSIWA. According to the ILC, selecting countermeasures is at the injured State's discretion, and it should select countermeasures that are reversible if it has a choice between a number of effective and lawful countermeasures.[31] This does not, however, mean that the injured State is totally free in its subjective appreciation; the test must always be that of proportionality. Even though the margin provided to injured States per the ILC has not been echoed by the ICJ and international tribunals yet, it may be embraced in their subsequent decisions. Nevertheless, it must be kept in mind that the ILC's

[25]Maurice Kamto, 'The Time Factor in the Application of Countermeasures', in: J. Crawford, A. Pellet & S. Olleson (eds), *The Law of International Responsibility* (New York: OUP, 2010) 1169, at 1174.

[26]For its customary character, see inter alia, Agnes G. Hurwitz, *The Collective Responsibility of States to Protect Refugees* (USA: OUP, 2009) at 204-206; David A. Martin 'Refugees and Migration', in: O. Schachter &. C. C. Joyner (eds) 1 *United Nations Legal Order* (CUP, 1995) 391, at 411; Jerzy Sztucki, 'The Conclusions on the International Protection of Refugees adopted by the Executive Committee of the UNHCR Programme', 1(3) *International Journal of Refugee Law* 285 (1989), at 300; Roman Boed, 'State of Necessity as a Justification for Internationally Wrongful Conduct', 3 *Yale Human Rights and Development Law Journal* 1 (2000), at 23.

[27]Convention Relating to the Status of Refugees, 28 July 1951, 189 U.N.T.S. 150, Art 33(1).

[28]Convention Against Torture and Other Cruel, Inhuman or Degrading Treatment or Punishment, 10 December 1984, 1465 U.N.T.S. 113, Art 3(1).

[29]OAU Convention Governing the Specific Aspects of Refugee Problems in Africa, 10 September 1969, 1001 U.N.T.S. 46, Art II(3).

[30]*Gabčíkovo-Nagymaros Project (Hungary v Slovakia),* ICJ Reports 1997, 7, para 87.

[31]ARSIWA Commentary, Art 49, para 9.

conceptualization of reversibility of countermeasures does not reflect the current case law.

Establishment of safe zones on a certain part of the Syrian territory on which the Assad government has lost its control for more than 5 years would probably be reversible since it would not have lasting effects under these circumstances. However, the intervening State[s] must make provisional the character of such establishments from the moment of their commencement.

2.1.6 Proportionality

In order for an injured State not to give rise to its responsibility due to its countermeasures, that State must always consider the test of proportionality. Proportionality is a well-established and widely recognized principle in State practice, jurisprudence of international courts and legal scholarship.[32] There is no doubt of the customary character of proportionality. The formulation of the proportionality requirement in Article 51 ARSIWA has been regarded as the customary statement of the rule: 'Countermeasures must be commensurate with the injury suffered, taking into account the gravity of the internationally wrongful act and the rights in question.'

The rationale behind the condition of proportionality in the adoption of countermeasures is repeatedly stated in ARSIWA as a safeguard against its abuse.[33] Furthermore, as has been indicated in the *Air Service Agreement* arbitration,[34] the requirement of proportionality serves to prevent escalation of the dispute through reactions. This risk emanates from the inherent, unilateral, and coercive nature of countermeasures.

As has been indicated by the tribunal in the *Air Service Agreement* arbitration,[35] by the ICJ in the *Gabčíkovo–Nagymaros Project* case,[36] and by the ILC in its Commentary to ARSIWA,[37] proportionality assessment must not purely depend on the quantitative element of the injury suffered. Qualitative aspects such as the significance of the interest protected by the rule breached and the seriousness of the infringement should also be taken into account. This has been clearly reflected in the wording of Article 51 ARSIWA, while it also addresses the gravity of the internationally wrongful act and the rights in question in addition to the injury

[32]ARSIWA, Commentary to Art 51 para 1.

[33]ARSIWA Commentary, Art 51, para 5; Part Three, Chap. 2 (Countermeasures) paras 2, 6.

[34]*Air Service Agreement of 27 March 1946* (US v. France), 18 RIAA 416 (1978), para 91.

[35]*Idem,* para 83.

[36]*Gabčíkovo-Nagymaros Project (Hungary v Slovakia),* ICJ Reports 1997, 7, paras 85, 87.

[37]ARSIWA Commentary, Art 51, paras 4, 6.

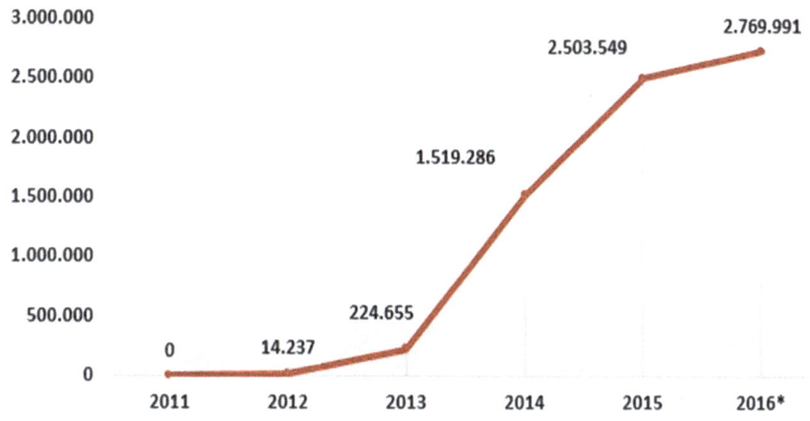

Fig. 2.1 Number of Syrians under temporary protection in Turkey per year as of 10 November 2016. *Source* Republic of Turkey Ministry of Interior Directorate General of Migration Management, *Temporary Protection*, available at: http://www.goc.gov.tr/icerik3/temporary-protection_915_1024_4748 [accessed: 14 November 2016]

suffered which is the primary element. Therefore, as has been indicated by O'Keefe,[38] the gravity of the internationally wrongful act and the rights in question should be seen as moral elements of the overall injury suffered. One may reach this conclusion simply by looking at the concept of injury in article 31(2) ARSIWA: 'injury includes any damage, whether material or moral, caused by the internationally wrongful act of a State.' In assessment of the moral damage, consideration of the scale and duration of the breach would be quite determinant.

In light of this explanation on material and moral damage, the damage that refugee-receiving States are exposed to may be better analyzed. For instance, Turkey has been receiving and hosting an ever-growing number of Syrian refugees, currently amounting to slightly fewer than three million, for longer than five years (Fig. 2.1).

The material damage of Syria's violation of its international obligations can be seen in its social, political, economic, and security burdens on Turkey. Massive flow of refugees from Syria to Turkey since 2011 seriously impairs the Turkish government's ability to maintain a stable and secure environment for its population and leaves the country vulnerable to terrorist attacks. In addition, the sudden presence of large numbers of individuals constitutes a real economic burden to the receiving country as Turkey is already home to lightly fewer than three million Syrian refugees and spends approximately $500 million on them monthly, creating

[38]Roger O'Keefe, 'Proportionality', in: J. Crawford, A. Pellet & S. Olleson (eds) *The Law of International Responsibility* (New York: OUP, 2010) 1157, at 1163.

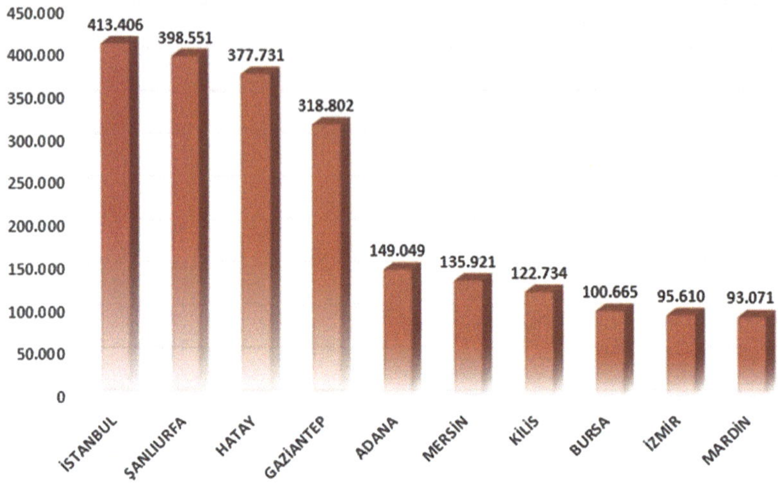

Fig. 2.2 Syrians under temporary protection in Turkey (Top 10 Provinces). *Source* Republic of Turkey Ministry of Interior Directorate General of Migration Management, *Temporary Protection*, available at: http://www.goc.gov.tr/icerik3/temporary-protection_915_1024_4748 [accessed: 14 November 2016]

a "black hole" for its economy.[39] Furthermore, there are serious social problems arising from the impact of Syrian refugees on the labor market and the altering demographic balance, particularly in some southern cities of Turkey such as Hatay, Gaziantep, Şanlıurfa, Kilis, Mardin, Mersin, and Adana.[40] In some south Turkish provinces near the Syrian border, the Syrian population has already outnumbered the native population. This is also a threat to the national composition of the country (Fig. 2.2).

In addition to those material damages, Turkey has suffered moral damage as it has been unable to exercise its sovereign right to determine who is allowed to enter its territory because of the Syrian refugee outflow.

An injured State does not have to take countermeasures that are in kind with the internationally wrongful act of a responsible State,[41] but not every desirable or useful means to protect the State's interest[s] can be considered within the scope of countermeasures. Such measures must first be shown to be necessary. The need for,

[39]Mehmet Cetingulec, 'How long can Turkey afford growing refugee bill?', *Al Monitor,* 26 April 2016, available at: http://www.al-monitor.com/pulse/originals/2016/05/turkey-syria-growing-refugee-bill.html [accessed: 12 July 2016].

[40]See, inter alia, Oytun Orhan & Sabiha Senyücel Gundogar, *Effects of the Syrian Refugees on Turkey*, January 2015, ORSAM Report No: 195, available at: http://www.orsam.org.tr/files/Raporlar/rapor195/195eng.pdf [accessed: 12 July 2016].

[41]ARSIWA Commentary, Part Three, Chap. 2, para 5.

and the possibility of, establishing a safe zone must be considered on a case-by-case basis since each refugee situation is unique.[42] The situation in Turkey clearly demonstrates how necessary a safe zone is to avert further outflow of refugees in the absence of any other means available. Furthermore, as Syria has been unable to prevent the large-scale influx of refugees from its territory violating Turkey's sovereignty, the intrusion of Turkish forces into Syria to establish a safe zone may be considered a proportionate countermeasure unless any less-intrusive measure would have the same effect on the prevention of influx of refugees. Consequently, I am of the opinion that in the event of the violation of its sovereignty, the injured State should be entitled to act in a way that violates the sovereignty of the State responsible for the violation. If the responsible State is unable to halt large-scale movement of people across international borders, then it must suffer the consequences of having the injured State take measures on its territory, including extraterritorial exercise of countermeasures.

Instead of having recourse to devastating measures against both the Syrian government and Syrian civilians, Turkey has long proposed the establishment of a safe zone in northern Syria near the Turkish border.[43] This brings the *Corfu Channel case* to mind in which the UK undertook a careful minesweeping operation instead of having resorted to naval blockades and bombardments of Albanian ports.[44] In a similar manner, temporary safe zones appear to be the least intrusive and proportionate response among other forcible measures on militarily destabilized countries in order to contribute to the settlement of the disputes within the context of refugee outflows.

The particular circumstances of Syria should be taken into account in any assessment of proportionality. The Syrian government has been unable to exercise control over the area stretching from Azaz to Jarablus near the border of Turkey for nearly five years. This area has long been proposed by Turkey for the establishment of a zone stretching along the Turkish border in Syria.[45] After Turkish Armed Forces launched Operation Euphrates Shield to clear DAESH, a widely recognized terrorist group active in Syria and Iraq, out from its southern border region on 24 August 2016, the Turkey-backed Syrian opposition regained the control of the all area from Azaz to Jarabulus on the 12th day of the operation, and DAESH presently controls no land along the Turkish border in Syria (Fig. 2.3). Under these circumstances, there is no measure less intrusive than the establishment of safe zones capable of both protecting Turkey's sovereign rights in the face of a large-scale

[42]B. S. Chimni, *supra* note 21, at 853.

[43]'President Erdoğan: Turkey to set up 5,000 sq km safe zone in Syria' *Daily Sabah*, 2 October 2016, available at: http://www.dailysabah.com/war-on-terror/2016/10/03/president-erdogan-turkey-to-set-up-5000-sq-km-safe-zone-in-syria.

[44]Theodore Christakis, 'Intervention and Self-help', in: K. Bannelier, T. Christakis & S. Heathcote (eds) *The ICJ and the Evolution of International Law: the Enduring Impact of the "Corfu Channel" Case* (London: Routledge, 2012) 211, at 212.

[45]Murat Sofuoglu, 'Safe zone' calls for Syrian refugees in an unsafe country', *TRTWORLD*, 25 April 2016 available at: http://www.trtworld.com/in-depth/safe-zone-calls-for-syrian-refugees-in-an-unsafe-country-93759 [accessed: 5 September 2016].

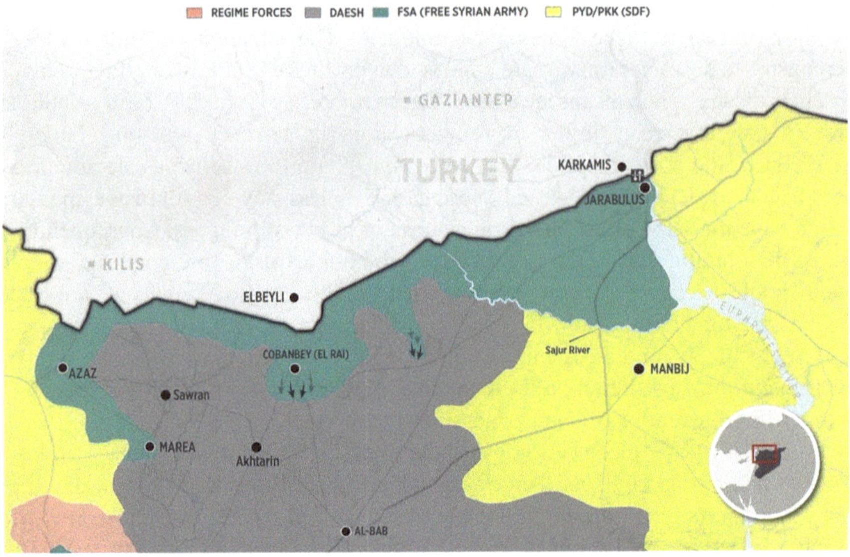

Fig. 2.3 Turkish border with Syria was cleared of DAESH after operation Euphrates shield. *Source* 'Security corridor in Azaz-Jarabulus expands,' *Anadolu Agency*, 6 September 2016, available at: http://aa.com.tr/en/info/infographic/1888 [accessed: 10 September 2016]

influx of refugees and providing safety to those who are fleeing conflict and violence in Syria. Since the international community has failed to persuade the Assad government through other means to ensure compliance with its international obligations, a safe zone seems the most acceptable solution for reducing refugee outflow by eliminating the need for flight.

Consequently, in the absence of other means of redress, there is a high degree of legal acceptability that the establishment of safe zones as a forcible countermeasure is a proportionate response to large-scale refugee outflows.[46]

2.2 Collective Countermeasures

In view of the wide range of grave breaches of obligations deriving from peremptory norms of international law and *erga omnes* obligations in Syria,[47] one may also argue for collective countermeasures. This is due to the fact that the vague

[46]Nicholas Tsagourias, 'Necessity and the Use of Force: A Special Regime', in I. F. Dekker and E. Hey (eds) 41 *Netherlands Yearbook of International Law* 11 (2010), at 25.

[47]UN Human Rights Council (UNHRC), 10th Report of the Independent International Commission of Inquiry on the Syrian Arab Republic (IICISAR), (2015), A/HRC/30/48, paras 168-173.

and imprecise formulation of Article 48 ARSIWA leaves the impression that any State could invoke any breach of *erga omnes* obligation to take countermeasures regardless of the gravity of the breach and regardless of whether that State is directly affected or not. This issue caused dissidence in the ILC's first reading since some members considered adoption of collective countermeasures as a risk of entanglement of Security Council powers with the individual reactions of States while others were of the counterview.[48] However, it cannot be interpreted in a manner that allows all States to react by means of countermeasures since such interpretation would be inconsistent with the realm of the Security Council's authority and State practice.[49] Since the Security Council has invoked its powers, deriving from Chapter VII, more frequently since the Cold War era, collective countermeasures taken on the individual level became more rare.[50] Besides, according to the traditional view of the law of international responsibility, perpetration of a wrongful act creates only bilateral consequences between the responsible State and the injured State.[51]

Even if collective countermeasures may be assumed to have a subsidiary character in relation to the powers of the Security Council in the face of violations of obligations representing a general interest, this is a rather gray area in international law. As has been indicated in the Commentary to Article 54, 'the current state of international law on countermeasures taken in the general or collective interest is uncertain.'[52] Moreover, as this book primarily focuses on the response of a State which is directly injured by a large-scale refugee influx and there is no value added from that State's perspective to the issue, collective countermeasures are not scrutinized here.

2.3 Forcible Countermeasures

The International Law Association (ILA), in the conclusion of its *Draft Report on Aggression and the Use of Force*,[53] sheds light on concerns of the international community regarding the failure to respond to changing forms of security threats. In *Oil Platforms*, Judge Simma,[54] in his separate opinion, stressed the crisis of the

---

[48]ILC *Yearbook* 1995/II/2, 48th Session, at 52.

[49]Linos-Alexandre Sicilianos 'Countermeasures in Response to Grave Violations of Obligations Owed to the International Community', in: J. Crawford, A. Pellet & S. Olleson (eds) *The Law of International Responsibility* (New York: OUP, 2010) 1137, at 1139.

[50]*Idem*, 1146.

[51]Dionisio Anzilotti, *Cours de droit international*, (tr G. Gidel, Paris: Sirey, 1929), at 467 cited in Linos-Alexandre Sicilianos, *supra* note 49, at 1137.

[52]ARSIWA Commentary, Art 54, para 6.

[53]International Law Association (ILA), Draft Report on Aggression and the Use of Force (Johannesburg Conference, May 2016) at 19.

[54]*Oil Platforms (US v Iran)*, ICJ Reports 2003, 1, at 328 para 6 (Judge Simma, sep op).

United Nations system of maintenance of peace and security, of which Articles 2(4) and 51 UN Charter are cornerstones. He further stated that the existing Charter Law becomes more controversial in the matter of further viability of the limits on unilateral military force. In this respect, large-scale refugee outflow from Syria to Turkey demonstrates the need for a unilateral right to use force preventively. This section attempts to survey the evidence that this need may be satisfied by interpreting countermeasures in a way that the State directly injured by the internationally wrongful act of the other is given the right to react through forcible countermeasures if its conditions are met. As has been explained below, pursuant to international customary law, general principles of law, as subsidiary means, judicial decisions, separate opinions, and the writing of scholars, such interpretation would not be in contradiction with the UN Charter as required in Article 59 ARSIWA.

2.3.1 *Character of the Use of Force*

According to Iwasawa and Iwatsuki,[55] the injured State is obliged to endeavor to settle disputes through amicable means and cannot resort to forcible countermeasures that are of unilateral and coercive nature. Articles 2(3) and 33 of the UN Charter, which impose the obligation to resolve disputes peacefully, can be referred to as a basis for this claim. The ILC's Draft Articles, hence, debar the injured State from taking countermeasures that are not in compliance with certain basic obligations, in particular the threat or use of force (Article 50(1)(a)) and peremptory norms (Article 50(1)(d)).

In Article 26 ARSIWA, the ILC stated that none of the circumstances listed under Chapter V precludes the wrongfulness of an act that is not in conformity with an obligation arising under a peremptory (*jus cogens*) norm. In its commentary, while citing 'the prohibitions of aggression, genocide, slavery, racial discrimination, crimes against humanity and torture, and the right to self-determination' as peremptory norms,[56] not mentioning the prohibition on the use of force has given rise to different opinions on the question of whether it is of peremptory character.[57]

Although Article 53 of the Vienna Convention on the Law of Treaties of 1969 defines the concept of peremptory norm, it does not provide a list of norms that have been recognized by all States as meeting the criteria set forth in that article.[58] Accordingly, there are certain rules of international law that the international community of States as a whole has agreed not only on their existence but also on

---

[55]Yuji Iwasawa and Naoki Iwatsuki, 'Procedureal Conditions', in: J. Crawford, A. Pellet & S. Olleson (eds) *The Law of International Responsibility* (New York: OUP, 2010) 1149, at 1152.

[56]ARSIWA Commentary, Art 26, para 6.

[57]Louise Arimatsu, 'The Law of State Responsibility in Relation to Border Crossings: An Ignored Legal Paradigm', 89 *International Law Studies* 21 (2013), at 48.

[58]Vienna Convention on the Law of Treaties, 23 May 1969, 1155 UNTS 331, Art 53.

their peremptory character. This means that no State can deviate from it unless a new rule of the same character emerges.

According to Corten,[59] the prohibition on the use of force is a part of international *jus cogens* and therefore cannot be circumvented by reference to exceptional circumstances and secondary rules such as necessity and countermeasures. He claims that the circumstances precluding wrongfulness could only be operative unless we enter the domain of the use of force within the meaning of Article 2(4) UN Charter. Despite this predominant view in international law doctrine that categorizes the prohibition on the use of force as a part of international *jus cogens*,[60] it is hard to find strong evidence in the form of explicit declarations on the part of States to support this view.[61] Furthermore, generally accepted exceptions of the prohibition on use of force enable a State to lawfully derogate from that rule. This is inconsistent with the definition of a peremptory norm.[62] Moreover, although the use of force is prohibited in Article 2(4), the question as to what constitutes a use of force remains uncertain since the Charter does not provide a definition or criteria.

Under such uncertainty and debates over its scope, one must question how the existence of a peremptory norm can be proved. If international law was only governed by Europe, it would be easier to establish new peremptory norms. However, with 194 States, one must be careful to claim that the prohibition on the use of force is a part of international *jus cogens*, since it is often the argument of the poor side which has no other argument.

2.3.2 The Ban on the Use of Force and Forcible Countermeasures

According to the predominant view, all uses of force are prohibited under the *jus ad bellum* regime save for the two codified exceptions in the UN Charter which are self-defense, recognized in Article 51, and forcible measures that are adopted or authorized by the Security Council under Chapter VII. In addition, a State may

---

[59]Olivier Corten, 'L'état de nécessité peut-ils justifier un recours à la force non constitutif d'agression?', 1 *The Global Community Yearbook of International Law & Jurisprudence* 11 (2004) cited in: Theodore Christakis, *supra* note 44, at 221.

[60]Albrecht Randelzhofer & Oliver Dörr, 'Article 2(4)', in: B. Simma et al. (eds) *The Charter of the United Nations: A Commentary* Vol. I (2nd edn, OUP, 2012) 200, at 231; Charles Leben, 'Obligations Relating to The Use of Force and Arising From Peremptory Norms of International Law', in: J. Crawford, A. Pellet & S. Olleson (eds.), *The Law of International Responsibility* (New York: OUP, 2010) 1177, at 1202.

[61]James Green, 'Questioning the Peremptory Status of the Prohibition of the Use of Force', 32 *Michigan Journal of International Law* 242 (2011), at 254.

[62]Ulf Linderfalk, 'The Effect of Jus Cogens Norms: Whoever Opened Pandora's Box, Did You Ever Think About the Consequences?', 18 *European Journal of International Law* 853 (2007), at 860.

consent to military operations by foreign forces on its territory.[63] Although none of these exceptions seem available to refugee-receiving State[s] to deal with the unwanted large-scale influx of Syrian refugees, it is claimed here that there are also countermeasures to which the prohibition on the use of force does not apply if we accept the gap between armed attack and use of force.

The ICJ in the *Nicaragua* case drew a distinction between an armed attack within the meaning of Article 51 of the Charter that is the most grave form of the use of force and the use of force of lesser degree of gravity by primarily taking scale and effects of the attack into account.[64] The Court reaffirmed that distinction based on a gravity threshold in its *Oil Platforms* case by stating that only the former qualifies as an armed attack.[65] Some commentators have concerns over accepting such a gap between armed attack(s) and use of force due to the fact that States may be encouraged to resort to force below the threshold of armed attack knowing that the other side cannot respond.[66] However, forcible countermeasures eliminate those concerns by recognizing the right to take proportionate defensive measures by force that is short of an armed attack against the responsible State's offensive hostile actions not reaching that threshold of armed attack.[67]

The ICJ, in *Nicaragua*,[68] recognized that the injured State is entitled to take proportionate countermeasures against the responsible State, but did not state whether those countermeasures can be forcible or not. Judge Simma, in *Oil Platforms*,[69] argues that this dictum of the Court cannot be understood as mere pacific reprisals, rather as defensive proportionate military action short of full-scale self-defense. According to Judge Simma,[70] it cannot be denied that the injured State has the right to resort to strictly proportionate defensive military measures against offensive military actions which remain below the threshold of an armed attack within the meaning of Article 51 UN Charter.

In addition to the terms *use of force* (Article 2(4)) and *armed attack* (Article 51), the UN Charter also uses the term *aggression* (Article 39) as triggering the Security Council's powers under Chapter VII. As the French version of the Charter uses the terms aggression and armed attack more or less identically, one may conclude that

---

[63]See, e.g., *Military and Paramilitary Activities in and against Nicaragua (Nicaragua v US)*, ICJ Reports 1986, 14, para 246.

[64]*Idem*, paras 194, 195.

[65]*Oil Platforms (US v Iran)*, ICJ Reports 2003, 1, paras 51, 64.

[66]James A. Green, *The International Court of Justice and Self-Defence in International Law* (Oxford: Hart Publishing, 2009), at 31–36.

[67]*Oil Platforms (US v Iran)*, ICJ Reports 2003, 1, at 331–333, paras 12–13 (Judge Simma, sep op).

[68]*Military and Paramilitary Activities in and against Nicaragua (Nicaragua v US)*, ICJ Reports 1986, 14, para 249.

[69]*Oil Platforms (US v Iran)*, ICJ Reports 2003, 1, at 332, para 12 (Judge Simma, sep op).

[70]*Idem*, at 331, para 12.

everything that is an act of aggression is also an armed attack.[71] However, as the ILA indicated in its *Draft Report on Aggression and the Use of Force*,[72] the relationship between aggression and armed attack is not clear. The Definition of Aggression,[73] adopted by the General Assembly in 1974 is accepted as reflecting customary international law. According to its Article 3(a), the presence of foreign forces without authorization of the territorial State would constitute an act of aggression. However, the ILC in its 1980 report stated that 'certain actions by States in the territory of other States which, although they may sometimes be of a coercive nature, serve only limited intentions and purposes bearing no relation to the purposes characteristic of a true act of aggression.'[74] Therefore, some limited temporary interventions of military forces with the aim of establishing safe zones on foreign territory, with no real gravity, to forestall further refugee influx by ensuring their safety within their country of origin where the territorial State has lost its control for a long time would not be of sufficient gravity to categorize it as aggression and/or armed attack.

Since Syria has been unable and unwilling to prevent the large-scale influx of refugees from its territory toward Turkey, the only way Turkey could avert further outflows was to take matters into its own hands which necessarily involves the violation of international law. However, the very use of armed forces truly with the aim of ensuring security of displaced persons, reducing refugee outflow by eliminating the need for flight as well as promoting international order by establishing safe zones, under these circumstances, would only qualify as use of force. Hence, on the basis of Judge Simma's separate opinion in *Oil Platforms case*, it may be claimed that Turkey has the right to establish safe zones, by force that is short of an armed attack, as a countermeasure against Syria's complete failure to carry out its duties under international law, namely protection of other States' rights on its own territory.

In my opinion, considering establishment of a safe zone as bringing into existence an international armed conflict would be going too far. This can be explained with the current example of Syria. The Syrian moderate opposition (Free Syrian Army) backed by Turkish armor, artillery, and jets has regained the whole land stretching from Azaz to Jarablus along Turkish border after the start of Operation Euphrates Shield which aims to keep that area safe from the terror groups of DAESH and PKK/PYD/YPG. During this military operation, Turkish armed forces have not come up against the Syrian regime forces, which lost the control of that area long ago. Considering such an operation under these circumstances bringing

[71]Wolff Heintschel von Heinegg, Lecture on 20 November 2015: Current Issues of the Law of Armed Conflict, Frankfurt (Oder), European University Viadrina.

[72]ILA, *supra* note 53, at 5.

[73]GA Res 3314(XXIX), 14 December 1974.

[74]ILC Report on the Work of its Thirty-Second Session, II(2) *ILC Yearbook* (1980), at 44.

into existence an international armed conflict between Turkey and Syria would not be in accordance with State practice as the ILA indicated in its *Final Report on the Meaning of Armed Conflict in International Law* that fighting of some intensity is required for all armed conflicts.[75] However, one may still consider such an operation for establishment and maintenance of safe zones bringing into existence an international armed conflict by relying on the ICTY's interpretation of relevant international law: 'the existence of armed force between [S]tates is sufficient of itself to trigger the application of international humanitarian law.'[76] Nevertheless, even if it brings into existence an international armed conflict, this is without prejudice to the legality of the establishment of safe zones under *jus ad bellum.*

2.3.3 Forcible Measures Against Large-Scale Refugee Outflows

Weiner draws attention to the fact that governments may make use of large-scale movements of persons as a way to put pressure on neighboring States,[77] although they may deny such intent. The issue of weaponization of refugees has also appeared in the past: Loescher says that a mass influx of refugees can be deliberately used by the sending State with the aim of undermining regional stability and specifically destabilizing strategic or political adversaries.[78] Weiner gives some historical examples[79]: for instance, the government of Haiti was accused of promoting the outflow of its citizens to Florida in order to compel the US to substantially increase its economic aid to Haiti in 1981. In addition, the underlying cause of the movement of Afghans to Pakistan in 1980s that resulted from Soviet pressure was considered an attempt to compel Pakistan to reach an agreement with the Afghan regime and cut its military aid to insurgents. Furthermore, Vietnam was accused of forcing Malaysia to accept Chinese refugees in order to destabilize that country. A current case in point is that General Philip M. Breedlove, North Atlantic Treaty Organization (NATO)'s 17th Supreme Allied Commander Europe, accused

---

[75]International Law Association, Final Report on the Meaning of Armed Conflict in International Law (The Hague Conference, 2010) at 2.

[76]See, inter alia, *Prosecutor v Tadić, Case,* No IT-94-1, Decision on Defence Motion for Interlocutory Appeal on Jurisdiction, para 70 (ICTY, 2 October 1995); *Prosecutor v* Mucić et al., Case No. IT-96-21-T, Judgement (Trial Chamber), para 184 (ICTY, 16 November 1998).

[77]Myron Weiner, 'Security, Stability, and International Migration', 17(3) *International Security* 91 (1992–3), at 100.

[78]Gil Loescher, 'Refugees as Grounds for International Action', in: E. Newman & J. van Selm (eds) *Refugee and forced displacement: International security, human vulnerability, and the state* (Tokyo: UNU Press, 2003) 31, at 35.

[79]Myron Weiner, *supra* note 77, at 100–101.

Russia and the Assad government of deliberately weaponizing Syrian refugees to destabilize the target State[s].[80]

Weiner, Gordenker, Dowty & Loescher are of the opinion that when refugees are being used as a weapon, the target State may invoke the right of self-defense.[81] However, in order to invoke the right of self-defense, that State must be exposed to an armed attack, defined by the ICJ as the most grave form of the use of force. It is true that the very large-scale influx of Syrian refugees across international borders has had quite negative effects, such as direct and indirect economic costs, negative social and cultural consequences, threats to security both internally and externally, and its broader effect on the fabric of global stability. In spite of all these negative effects and threats, it is still very difficult for refugee-receiving State[s], even including Turkey which has the largest refugee population in the world,[82] to consider this influx an armed attack given the lack of consistent State practice indicating that it reaches the threshold of the most grave form of use of force.

Loescher claims that a large-scale refugee outflow is increasingly accepted as grounds for an armed intervention.[83] The justification of such intervention is claimed to be found in the actions of the State that compel persons to leave in a manner that threatens regional peace and security and therefore internationalizes its internal affairs.[84] Therefore, Dowty & Loescher claim that deriving a right to international action, including armed intervention, from the failure of a State in preventing a large-scale influx of persons from its territory toward another country would be a reasonable extension of customary law.[85] The reason why customary international law has no apparent specific rule on the issue of large-scale movements of people across international borders is that it has only recently become a frequent problem in inter-State relations.

In conclusion, my perspective is that it is possible to rely on State practice and interpret the relevant international law provisions governing military actions abroad in a way that does not prevent a State from establishing safe zones on the territory of a refugee-generating country on the grounds of countermeasures, as long as the required conditions are met.

---

[80]Lizzie Dearden, 'Russia and Syria 'weaponising' refugee crisis to destabilise Europe, Nato commander claims', *Independent*, 3 March 2016, available at: http://www.independent.co.uk/news/world/middle-east/russia-and-syria-weaponising-refugee-crisis-to-destabilise-europe-nato-commander-claims-a6909241.html [accessed: 12 July 2016].

[81]Leon Gordenker, *Refugees in International Politics* (New York: Columbia University Press, 1987) at 188–189; Myron Weiner (ed), *International Migration and Security* (Boulder, CO: Westview Press, 1993) at 8–9; Alan Dowty & Gil Loescher, 'Refugee Flows as Grounds for International Action', 21/1 *International Security* 43 (1996), at 50.

[82]European Commission Humanitarian Aid and Civil Protection, *Turkey: Refugee Crisis*, September 2016, at 1, available at: http://ec.europa.eu/echo/files/aid/countries/factsheets/turkey_syrian_crisis_en.pdf [accessed: 9 September 2016].

[83]Gil Loescher, *supra* note 78, at 32.

[84]Alan Dowty & Gil Loescher, *supra* note 81, at 59.

[85]*Idem*, at 45.

Chapter 3
Application of the Concept of Necessity to Justify the Establishment of Safe Zones to Prevent Large-Scale Refugee Outflows

Hugo Grotius,[1] considered the 'father of international law,' noted in the seventeenth century that the right to self-preservation existed in many States' internal law and would also be equally applicable to inter-State relations. This appears to be the first doctrine of necessity in the literature. Since there is no general conventional provision to anchor the rule, doubts have been expressed as to whether necessity constitutes a grounds for precluding wrongfulness concerning any act that is inconsistent with an international obligation.[2] However, the customary status of necessity has, in principle, been expressly recognized by a growing number of cascs, whilc at thc samc timc rcjccting its application to thc circumstanccs at hand. Three principle cases in which the plea of necessity has been raised are *Gabčíkovo–Nagymaros Project*,[3] the Advisory Opinion on the *Legal Consequences of the Construction of a Wall in the Occupied Palestinian Territory*,[4] and the decision of the ICSID tribunal in *CMS Gas Transmission v Argentina*.[5]

[1]Hugo Grotious, De Jure Belli ac Pacis Libri Tres Bk. II, Ch. I, Para. XII, Cl. 3 (1901, tr A.C. Campbell) cited in Roman Boed, 'State of Necessity as a Justification for Internationally Wrongful Conduct', 3 *Yale Human Rights and Development Law Journal* 1 (2000), at 4.
[2]*Rainbow Warrior (New Zealand v France)* 20 RIAA 215 (1990), at 254.
[3]*Gabčíkovo-Nagymaros Project (Hungary v Slovakia),* ICJ Reports 1997, 7.
[4]*Legal Consequences of the Construction of a Wall in the Occupied Palestinian Territory, Advisory Opinion,* ICJ Reports 2004, 136.
[5]*CMS Gas Transmission Company v Argentine Republic*, 14 ICSID Reports 152 (2005).

L.B. Çetinkaya, *Safe Zone*, SpringerBriefs in Law,
DOI 10.1007/978-3-319-51997-5_3

3.1 Analysis of the Requirements for a Necessity Defense to Establish of Safe Zones

The clear reference of the ICJ in the case concerning *Gabčíkovo–Nagymaros Project* to Draft Article 33 and its commentary adopted by the ILC on first reading in 1996,[6] and recognition of this formulation as a reflection of customary law, demonstrates how the ILC's work on necessity has been regarded as authoritative. The essence of Draft Article 33 of first reading in 1996 is reflected in Article 25 ARSIWA with slight language modifications.

Since necessity is a highly subjective defense, it is open to abuses and misuses that threaten legal stability. Because of this threat, the ILC formulated the concept of necessity with negation to emphasize its exceptional character.[7] Thus, specific and strict criteria, which are claimed by the ICJ as reflecting customary international law,[8] must be met holistically in order for a State to be able to invoke necessity in defense of establishment of safe zones.

3.1.1 An 'Essential Interest' of the State Must Be at Stake

The practice of international adjudicative bodies, as surveyed by the ILC's former Special Rapporteur Ago,[9] demonstrates that the plea of necessity had been considered only with regard to preservation of a State's very existence in the past. However, today's predominant view broadens the scope to include essential interests other than threats to a State's very existence, as can be seen in such cases as *Forests of Central Rhodope,*[10] *Properties of Bulgarian Minorities in Greece,*[11] and *Rights of Nationals of the United States of America in Morocco.*[12] The *Torrey Canyon* incident also offers an example. In 1967, Britain bombed a leaking Liberian tanker in order to burn off all oil remaining on board. The ILC ruled that the threat to the English coast and its population posed by the tanker was sufficient to preclude wrongfulness.[13] In this case, the danger of the oil spill posed a threat to one of the State's interests, namely the protection of the marine and coastal environment,

---

[6]*Gabčíkovo-Nagymaros Project (Hungary v Slovakia)*, (1997) ICJ Reports 7, paras 50–51.

[7]*Idem*, para 51.

[8]*Ibid.*

[9]Roberto Ago, 'Addendum to the eighth report on State responsibility' II (1) *ILC Yearbook* 13 (1980), paras 22 and 26 (pointing to the cases of *Russian Indemnity* and *French Company of Venezuela Railroads*).

[10]*Forests of Central Rhodope (Greece v. Bulgaria),* 3 UNRIAA 1405 (1933).

[11]*Properties of the Bulgarian Minorities in Greece*, II(2) *ILC Yearbook* 34 (1980).

[12]*Rights of Nationals of the United States of America in Morocco (France v US)*, ICJ Reports 1952, 176.

[13]ILC Report on the Work of its Thirty-Second Session, II(2) *ILC Yearbook* (1980), para. 15.

but not to the very existence of the Great Britain. Hence, *The Torrey Canyon* incident is significant in its conclusion that a State may invoke the necessity plea when one of its essential interests is threatened. The ICJ is of the same opinion as has been indicated in the case concerning *Gabčíkovo–Nagymaros Project.*[14]

The question at hand, therefore, is the following: what constitutes an essential interest of a State? This is definitely not a fixed category since the specific circumstances of each case need to be taken into account to determine whether a State's threatened interest is essential. Ago enumerates 'political or economic survival, the continued functioning of [a State's] essential services, the maintenance of internal peace, the survival of a sector of its population, [and] the preservation of the environment of its territory or a part thereof' to exemplify the interests which may reach the threshold of essential interest within the meaning of the ILC's formulation.[15]

Heathcote draws attention to the difficulty in finding the limits of a State's discretion in determining whether or not the protection of such an interest is indeed essential.[16] Certain social consensus among the international community or the State's domestic jurisdiction appears as two possible arguments. However, as the question of whether a given interest is essential depends on the circumstances of a case and cannot be prejudged, it is impossible to place preset limitations upon the State's discretion. Therefore, instead of trying to specify the limits of the State's discretion, it would be more reasonable and more important to ascertain whether sufficiently extreme circumstances existed for a State to rely on the necessity plea. Consequently, there is no specific criterion for limiting the State's discretion in the determination of an interest as essential. However, it does not mean that States are unrestricted in this assessment. On the contrary, all the circumstances must be taken into account to determine the extent to which a given interest is essential.[17] Hence, it must be determined on a case-by-case basis.

A State may consider a large-scale influx of refugees as a threat to its essential interests, such as protection of the environment or the preservation of internal order and security. For instance, after welcoming 500,000 Rwandan refugees in 1994, Tanzania changed its policy by closing its borders to refugees in 1995. Tanzania's Deputy Home Affairs Minister Mwambulukutu explained this policy change by reasoning that: 'Protecting and assisting refugees has brought new risks to national security, exacerbated tensions between [S]tates and caused extensive damage to the environment…'.[18]

---

[14]*Gabčíkovo-Nagymaros Project (Hungary v Slovakia)*, ICJ Reports 1997, 7, para 53.

[15]Roberto Ago, *supra* note 9, para. 2.

[16]Sarah Heathcote, 'Circumstances Precluding Wrongfulness in the ILC Articles on State Responsibility: Necessity', in: J. Crawford, A. Pellet and S. Olleson (eds), *The Law of International Responsibility* (New York: OUP, 2010) 491, at 497.

[17]ARSIWA Commentary, Art 25, para 15.

[18]Augustine Mahiga, 'A Change of Direction for Tanzania', 110 *Refugees Magazine* 14 (1997), at 14.

The maintenance of internal order, security, and stability needs to be considered as one of the essential interest[s] that may be jeopardized by a sudden presence of large-scale number of refugees. Boed points to probable destabilizing social and economic effects of a sudden mass influx of refugees by referring to substantial burdens on the administrative structure, such as proper registration of arriving individuals, provision of food and shelter, maintenance of security and peace, and provision of medical and social care.[19] Loescher lists possible effects of a large-scale refugee influx: direct and indirect economic costs, negative social, and cultural consequences, threats to security both internally and externally, and its broader effect on the fabric of global stability.[20]

ARSIWA Commentary specifically mentions ensuring safety of a civilian population among a wide variety of interests.[21] The large-scale flow of refugees from Syria to Turkey since 2011 may well be deemed a threat to Turkey's essential interests by leaving the country vulnerable to terrorist attacks and seriously impairing the Turkish government's ability to maintain a stable and secure environment for its population. This may be more determinant among other effects of refugees on receiving countries to understand why States and their citizens often have an aversion to such movements.[22] Because of the failure of the Assad government to exercise due diligence over its borders within the context of large-scale refugee outflow, Turkey has struggled to identify and catch terror suspects, among nearly three million Syrian refugees, affiliated to DAESH, a widely recognized terrorist group active in Syria and Iraq, or PKK which is on the terrorist list of several States and international organizations including NATO and EU as a terrorist group active in Turkey, or PKK's Syrian branch PYD and its armed wing YPG.[23] Those groups are claimed to be responsible for bomb attacks throughout Turkey, including Ankara, Istanbul, and areas close to the Syrian border such as Gaziantep and Şanlıurfa.[24] As Turkey shares a very long border with Syria (911 km/559.2 mile) that has been used by refugees to enter into and egress from its territory, it has been

[19]Roman Boed, *supra* note 1, at 26.

[20]Gil Loescher, 'Refugees as Grounds for International Action', in: E. Newman and J. van Selm (eds) *Refugee and forced displacement: International security, human vulnerability, and the state* (Tokyo: UNU Press, 2003) 31, at 33.

[21]ARSIWA Commentary, Art 25, para 14.

[22]Myron Weiner, 'Security, Stability, and International Migration', 17(3) *International Security* 91 (1992–3), at 95.

[23]Some States, such as the US, ignore the link between PKK and PYD/YPG and do not recognize PYD/YPG as a terror group for pragmatic reasons in the fight against the DAESH terrorist group. However, the strong link between PYD/YPG and PKK is one of the most well known facts over Syria. See, inter alia, 'Terrorist PKK, PYD are 'exactly same thing,' says Barzani', *TRTWORLD*, 23 March 2016, available at: http://www.trtworld.com/mea/terrorist-pkk-pyd-are-exactly-same-thing-says-barzani-73972 [accessed: 12 July 2016].

[24]See, Kılıç Bugra Kanat, 'DAESH and PKK attack Turkey again', *Daily Sabah*, 21 August 2016, available at: http://www.dailysabah.com/columns/kilic-bugra-kanat/2016/08/21/daesh-and-pkk-attack-turkey-again [accessed: 21 August 2016].

an uphill struggle for Turkey to identify and catch terror suspects in the absence of Syrian authorities' willingness and ability to do the same on its own territory.

In addition, the sudden presence of large numbers of individuals constitutes a real economic burden to the receiving country as Turkey is already home to almost three million Syrian refugees incurring a monthly spend of $500 million. This spending have been called an economic 'black hole.'[25] Furthermore, there are serious social problems arising from the impact of Syrian refugees on the labor market and the altering demographic balance in some cities in southern Turkey, particularly Hatay, Gaziantep, Şanlıurfa, Kilis, Mardin, Mersin, and Adana.[26] In some south Turkish provinces near Syrian border, the Syrian population has already outnumbered the native population. This is also a threat to the national composition of the country.

Turkey may excuse its noncompliance with its international duty not to violate the territorial sovereignty of Syria by asserting that the large-scale influx of refugees has jeopardized its economic, political, and social stability, as well as the maintenance of the order and security of its community. In conclusion, by considering social, political, economic, and security burdens of large-scale influx of refugees from Syria to Turkey since 2011, it would be advisable for Turkey to claim that its essential interests are at stake.

3.1.2 *Presence of a 'Grave and Imminent Peril'*

The necessity justification may be invoked in situations where States encounter grave and imminent threat to their essential interests. Although both the precedents of the ICJ and the advice of the ILC require a peril to be grave,[27] neither provides any measure of gravity. However, it would be consistent with the aim of the necessity plea to say that any threat likely to seriously impair a State's ability to realize its essential interest can be considered a grave peril. According to this perspective, unless compelling evidence of a grave and imminent threat by a large-scale influx of refugees can be demonstrated, Turkey would not be able to invoke the necessity plea to justify its envisioned safety zone in Syria. As a large-scale flow of refugees from Syria to Turkey since 2011 leaves the country vulnerable to terrorist attacks and seriously impairs the Turkish government's

---

[25]Mehmet Cetingulec, 'How long can Turkey afford growing refugee bill?', *Al Monitor,* 26 April 2016, available at: http://www.al-monitor.com/pulse/originals/2016/05/turkey-syria-growing-refugee-bill.html [accessed: 12 July 2016].

[26]See, inter alia, Oytun Orhan and Sabiha Senyücel Gundogar, *Effects of the Syrian Refugees on Turkey*, January 2015, ORSAM Report No: 195, available at: http://www.orsam.org.tr/files/Raporlar/rapor195/195eng.pdf [accessed: 12 July 2016].

[27]*Gabčíkovo-Nagymaros Project (Hungary v Slovakia),* ICJ Reports 1997, 7, para 52; ARSIWA Commentary, Art 25, para 15.

ability to maintain a stable and secure environment for its population, the peril may well be deemed grave.

The intention behind the choice of the word 'peril' is indicated by the ICJ in the case concerning *Gabčíkovo–Nagymaros Project*, where it details both the damage which has already materialized but also includes the notion of risk.[28] Heathcote, therefore, emphasises the preventative character of the necessity plea which aims to 'manage crises which if not averted, will lead to grave harm.'[29] According to this approach, a State may invoke necessity after receiving massive numbers of individuals, but also shortly before an influx occurs in order to avert it. However, the peril has to be 'imminent' in the sense of proximate. The ICJ indicated that it might still be considered imminent even if the realization of that peril appears in the long term providing that it is clearly established on the basis of the evidence reasonably available at the time.[30] The condition of imminent peril was interpreted by Ago as 'a present danger to the threatened interest.'[31]

In light of this information, it would not be wrong to say that Turkey may have relied on state of necessity as a preventative mechanism as early as 2014 when the numbers of Syrian refugees dramatically increased (see Fig. 3.1), providing a realization of danger to Turkey's public order and security in response to the influx was sufficiently established on the basis of the evidence available at the time. Besides, the numbers of Syrian refugees and their social, political, economic, and security burden on Turkey entitles the invocation of the necessity plea in order to cope with the refugee issue since grave peril exists.

3.1.3 The State Must Have no Other Means of Safeguarding Its Interest

This criterion reflects the exceptional character of the necessity plea by requiring specific measures to be taken by a State to protect its essential interest and they must be the sole means at its disposal. In other words, state of necessity cannot be invoked while there are other means available to safeguard that interest even if they may be more costly or less convenient.[32]

While States have the right to respond to a large-scale influx of refugees toward their countries in order to be able to maintain a stable and secure environment for their population, the measure of establishment of a safe zone against the State within which the refugee flow is generated is bound to remain consistent with applicable

[28]*Gabčíkovo-Nagymaros Project (Hungary v Slovakia)*, ICJ Reports 1997, 7, para 54.

[29]Sarah Heathcote, *supra* note 16, at 497.

[30]*Gabčíkovo-Nagymaros Project (Hungary v Slovakia)*, ICJ Reports 1997, 7, para 51; ARSIWA Commentary, Art 25, para 16.

[31]Roberto Ago, *supra* note 9, para 13.

[32]ARSIWA Commentary, Art 25, para 15.

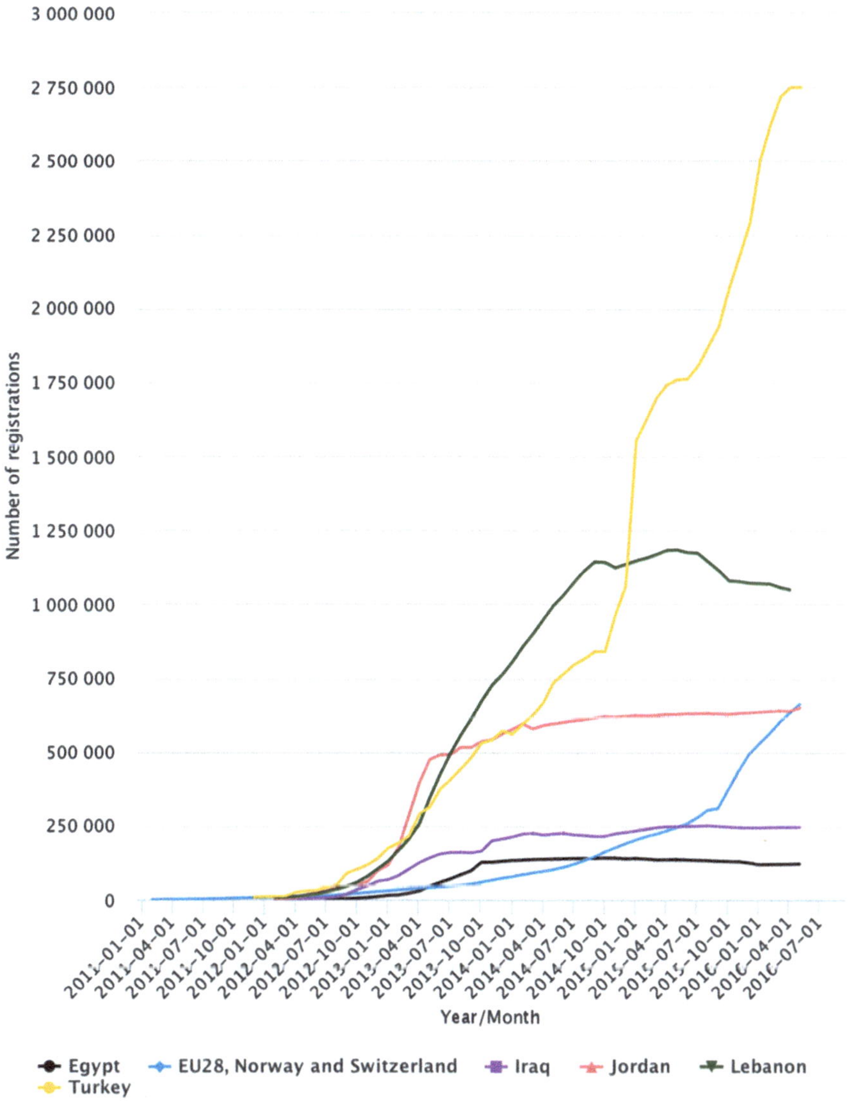

Fig. 3.1 Registered Syrian refugees by country of asylum as of 1 May 2016. *Source* Migration Policy Centre, *Registered Syrian refugees by country of asylum,* (data taken from Eurostat [EU28, Norway and Switzerland]; UNHCR [Turkey, Lebanon, Jordan, Iraq, and Egypt]) available at: http://www.migrationpolicycentre.eu/migrant-crisis/focus-on-syrians/ [accessed: 4 September 2016]

international law. Thus, it is discussed here whether the safe zone is the only means at the disposal of a refugee-receiving country, in other words, whether there are lawful alternatives available to the refugee-receiving State to protect its essential interest against a large-scale influx of refugees across international borders.

3.1.3.1 Resettlement of Refugees in Third States

The first alternative to safe zones may be seeking resettlement of refugees in third States. Since the issue here is not about small numbers, but rather millions of refugees, no country accepts such a burden on its own. However, States may be willing to share that burden by hosting refugees in their countries for various purposes such as to satisfy a need for cheap labor, to lower the average age of the population with younger migrants, or to embrace those in need of assistance for purely humanitarian reasons. Nonetheless, in the case of Syrian refugees in Turkey, reluctance of third States to accept them to their countries is one of the most well-known facts in the world today, as one can see in the failed refugee deal between the European Union and Turkey. Under these circumstances, resettlement of Syrian refugees in third countries would not be considered an alternative means available to Turkey.

3.1.3.2 Refugee Camps/Accommodation Centers in the Refugee-Receiving Country

The second alternative to safe zones may be setting up refugee camps in the refugee-receiving country. If we were talking about some hundreds of thousands of refugees, it would make sense to argue that setting up such accommodation centers constitutes a viable option. However, in order to understand better what the total number of Syrian refugees in Turkey means, it may be seen as half of the populations of Singapore, Denmark, or Finland; as almost equal to populations of Armenia and Lithuania; or as larger than the populations of Qatar and Slovenia.[33] Even if it were possible to establish camps sufficient for that number of refugees and to bring them together in those areas, the economic burden on the government would definitely be unaffordable. It is clear that those camps operate as the first place in which Syrian refugees temporarily stay until they find a place in city centers. In Turkey, two and a half million refugees live in several cities not only with the financial support of the government, but also earn their own living. Only one-tenth of them stay in camps. Keeping almost three million refugees in camps for an unknown period is simply impossible. In addition to the unaffordable economic burden, it would simply not be a feasible solution to address overwhelming flow of refugees. Instead of preventing further refugee flows, it may even attract more refugees in the country. Therefore, this does not constitute an alternative means available to Turkey to cope with the large-scale influx of refugees (Fig. 3.2).

[33]The World Bank Group, Overview per country, available at: http://data.worldbank.org/indicator/SP.POP.TOTL [accessed: 4 September 2016].

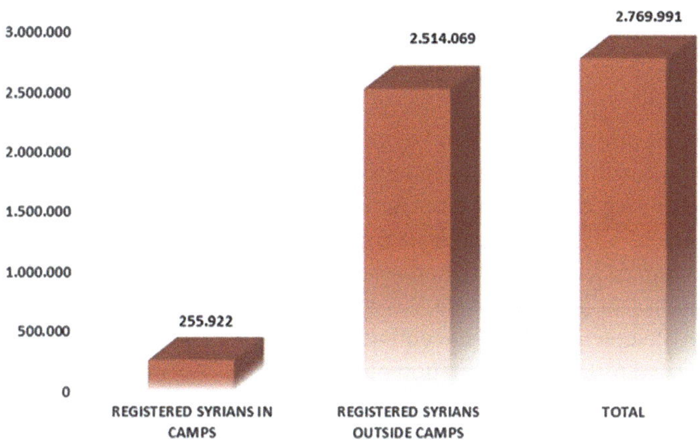

Fig. 3.2 Syrians under temporary protection in Turkey staying in and outside of accommodation centers as of 10 November 2016. *Source* Republic of Turkey Ministry of Interior Directorate General of Migration Management, *Temporary Protection,* available at: http://www.goc.gov.tr/icerik3/temporary-protection_915_1024_4748 [accessed: 14 November 2016]

3.1.3.3 Border Closure

The third alternative to safe zones may be rejection of displaced persons who are in search of safety by sealing borders. However, it is practically impossible to completely seal all borders unilaterally to prevent unwanted flows of individuals. Therefore, the effectiveness of border closure has long been controversial since it is rarely wholly effective even in the case of islands.[34] States vary in their capacity to control their borders against the intrusion of hundreds of thousands of refugees infiltrating across an international border in search of safety. States that are capable of defending themselves against wide range military attacks via missile, tank, and infantry are often unable to defend their sovereign rights in the face of a large-scale movement of persons toward their borders.[35] If a neighboring country has long borders, like Turkey's very long border (911 km–559.2 mile) with Syria, it becomes even more difficult to effectively implement a border closure policy.

Even if it is effectively implemented, which is very rare, border closure would mean re-exposing individuals to the gross human rights violations that drove them from their homes and turning a blind eye to this situation. Returning individuals to the imminent risk of persecution would entail violation of the *non-refoulement* rule, enshrined in many instruments such as Article 33(1) 1951 Refugee Convention,[36]

[34]See, inter alia, Myron Weiner, *supra* note 22, at 97.

[35]*Ibid.*

[36]Convention Relating to the Status of Refugees, 28 July 1951, 189 U.N.T.S. 150, Art 33(1).

Article 3(1) Convention Against Torture[37] and Article II(3) OAU Convention Governing the Specific Aspects of Refugee Problems in Africa.[38] Although those provisions do not explicitly deal with the issue of rejection from frontiers, as has been indicated by Goodwin-Gill,[39] there has been a growing consensus that the *non-refoulement* principle may also be applicable to individuals who have not yet arrived on the territory of the neighboring State. Martin also made the same statement by relying on State practice since 1951, and further, he argued its customary character.[40] The *non-refoulement* principle has been interpreted by many reputable academics to encompass non-rejection at the border, and it may be argued that this interpretation has attained the status of international customary law.[41] Authoritative statements of the Executive Committee of the UNHCR on several occasions attested to such interpretation of the principle.[42] Since the effects of both rejection at the border and closure of the border on displaced persons are the same, Boed concludes that the principle of *non-refoulement* does not allow a State to close its borders to those fleeing conflict and violence.[43]

In conclusion, it would not be realistic for a refugee-receiving State such as Turkey, which has a very long border with its neighboring refugee-generating State, to close its borders. Moreover, border closure is not a lawful alternative under these circumstances due to the fact that its implementation would be a violation of the principle of *non-refoulement*, which is of customary character.

3.1.3.4 Establishment of Safe Zones in the Refugee-Generating Country

The idea of a safe zone was first proposed in 1985 by Thailand which, as a developing country, was becoming increasingly attractive to displaced persons in its near abroad, to the Asian-African Legal Consultative Committee to analyze the

[37]Convention Against Torture and Other Cruel, Inhuman or Degrading Treatment or Punishment, 10 December 1984, 1465 U.N.T.S. 113, Art 3(1).

[38]OAU Convention Governing the Specific Aspects of Refugee Problems in Africa, 10 September 1969, 1001 U.N.T.S. 46, Art II(3).

[39]Guy S. Goodwin-Gill, *The Refugee in International Law* (2nd edn, New York: Clarendon Press, 1996) at 196.

[40]David A. Martin 'Refugees and Migration', in: O. Schachter and. C. C. Joyner (eds) 1 *United Nations Legal Order* (CUP, 1995) 391, at 411.

[41]See, inter alia, Guy S. Goodwin-Gill, *supra* note 39, at 196.

[42]Jerzy Sztucki, 'The Conclusions on the International Protection of Refugees adopted by the Executive Committee of the UNHCR Programme', 1(3) *International Journal of Refugee Law* 285 (1989), at 300.

[43]Roman Boed, *supra* note 1, at 23.

possibility of establishing safe zones for refugees and displaced persons in their country of origin.[44]

In 1993, the UN Security Council declared safe zones in Bosnia and authorized the United Nations Protection Force (UNPROFOR) for the protection of those zones.[45] However, Bosnian Muslims in those so-called safe zones were either executed or forced to flee by Serb forces in the absence of capability or willingness on the part of the UNPROFOR to create the conditions that would have guaranteed protection.[46] Such a zone was also established in Rwanda, again with authorization of the Security Council.[47] Although establishment of a safe zone in south-west Rwanda saved the lives of many hundreds of people, Chimni sharply criticizes allowing French troops, instead of the United Nations Assistance Mission for Rwanda (UNAMIR),[48] to initially establish that zone due to the fact that France had a previous relationship with the Hutu government leading to suspicion about France's role in the zone and encouragement for Hutus to flee instead of staying in that zone. Both of these examples have been widely seen as instances of failure by the international community to adopt such measures properly and in a timely manner.

The failure of States to take appropriate measures against humanitarian emergencies such as that in Rwanda in a timely manner was not legal or conceptual; rather as Kofi Annan pointed out, it was due to the reluctance of States to pay the human and other costs of intervention, and to doubts as to whether the use of force would be successful.[49] The failure to provide sufficient ground forces to Bosnia for protection of safe zones was based on similar reasons. As long as outside powers abstain from demonstrating their willingness and capacity to take all appropriate measures, including use of military force, to protect safe zones, this measure must not be taken in an effort to not repeat the tragedy of Bosnian safe zones. Therefore, beside the question of legality of establishment of safe zones, it must be noted here that this measure must be taken only when outside powers are willing and prepared to provide supplies and use military force in the defense of safe zones when needed.

As Haitian and Cuban governments were apparently unwilling to patrol the beaches to avert large-scale flows of their citizens by sea from their territories to the US in the early 1990s, the US established safe zone facilities first in the US naval

---

[44]B. S. Chimni, 'The Incarceration of Victims: Deconstructing Safety Zones', in: N. Al-Nauimi and R. Meese (eds), *International Legal Issues Arising Under the United Nations Decade of International Law* (The Netherlands: Martinus Nijhoff Publishers, 1995) 823, at 852.

[45]See, SC Resolutions 819 of 16 April 1993, 824 of 6 May 1993, 836 of 4 June 1993, 844 of 18 June 1993, 859 of 24 August 1993.

[46]Myron Weiner and Münz Rainer, 'Migrants, refugees and foreign policy: prevention and intervention strategies', 18(1) *Third World Quarterly* 25 (1997), at 39.

[47]See, SC Resolutions 918 of 17 May 1994, 925 of 8 June 1994, 929 of 22 June 1994.

[48]B. S. Chimni, *supra* note 44, at 851.

[49]Kofi A. Annan, Preventing war and disaster: a growing global challenge—Annual Report on the Work of the Organization, (New York: United Nations Department of Public Information, 1999), at 21.

base at Guantanamo Bay in Cuba and then in Panama. The US started to transport both Haitian and Cuban rafters to those facilities and declared that they will not be permitted to enter US territory unless they returned to their home country where they could then apply to US consular officials for refugee status or admission as immigrants. After effective implementation of this policy, the influx from both countries dramatically declined. This is an example of an external safe zone that would not be available to most countries that do not have offshore facilities comparable to the US bases in Panama and Guantanamo.[50]

In the face of the unwanted Kurdish refugee flow from Iraq to Turkey after the Gulf War, Turkey used its troops in prevention of their movement in order not to add those refugees to its own Kurdish population. The US, Great Britain and other allies used their military power to ensure the safety of Iraqi Kurds in northern Iraq against the Iraqi government by closing the safe zone to Iraqi troops, administration, and airplanes. By virtue of that protection, Kurds in Iraq and an estimated 1.5 million Kurds who had fled to Iran and Turkey came together in northern Iraq.[51] This case offers a successful example of the use of force to deal with an unwanted refugee flow.

As the experience in northern Iraq proved that the objective of preventing refugee flow could be successfully achieved by creating safe zones, Turkey has consistently proposed the establishment of safe zones in Syria.[52] There have been various predictions on the dimensions of the possible safe zone in Syria. For instance, according to some media reports, such a zone will be in a 90 km long and 40 km deep (55 mile by 25 mile) area stretching along the Turkish border between the northern Syrian towns of Marea and Jarablus.[53] Although its dimensions vary in different media reports, a rough sketch of the proposed safe zone can be seen in Fig. 3.3. The proximity of the proposed safe zone may enable the international community to deliver the humanitarian aid on the ground for Syrian refugees in that zone.

Turkish Armed Forces launched Operation Euphrates Shield to repel DAESH from its southern border region on 24 August 2016, and the Turkey-backed Syrian opposition regained the control of the area stretching from Azaz to Jarabulus on the 12th day of the operation. Turkey also declared the Euphrates River as its red line for the presence of Kurdish PKK/PYD/YPG. Turkish foreign minister Cavusoglu said that: 'Otherwise, I am saying very clearly that we will do what is necessary.'[54]

---

[50]Myron Weiner and Münz Rainer, *supra* note 46, at 37.

[51]Myron Weiner, *supra* note 22, at 124.

[52]Humeyra Pamuk and Seda Sezer, 'At G20 meeting, Turkey pushes plan for "safe zone" in Syria', *Reuters*, 5 September 2016, available at: http://in.reuters.com/article/g20-turkey-syria-idINKCN11B1FF [accessed: 9 September 2016].

[53]Euan McKirdy, Jason Hanna and Isil Sariyuce, 'Turkey sends tanks into Syria against ISIS; rebels reportedly capture town' *CNN*, 24 August 2016, available at: http://edition.cnn.com/2016/08/24/middleeast/turkish-troops-isis-syria-operation/index.html [accessed: 4 September 2016].

[54]Diyar Guldogan, 'Syrian operation is to clear Daesh, says Turkish FM' *Anadolu Agency*, 24 August 2016, available at: http://aa.com.tr/en/politics/syrian-operation-is-to-clear-daesh-says-turkish-fm-/634440 [accessed: 5 September 2016].

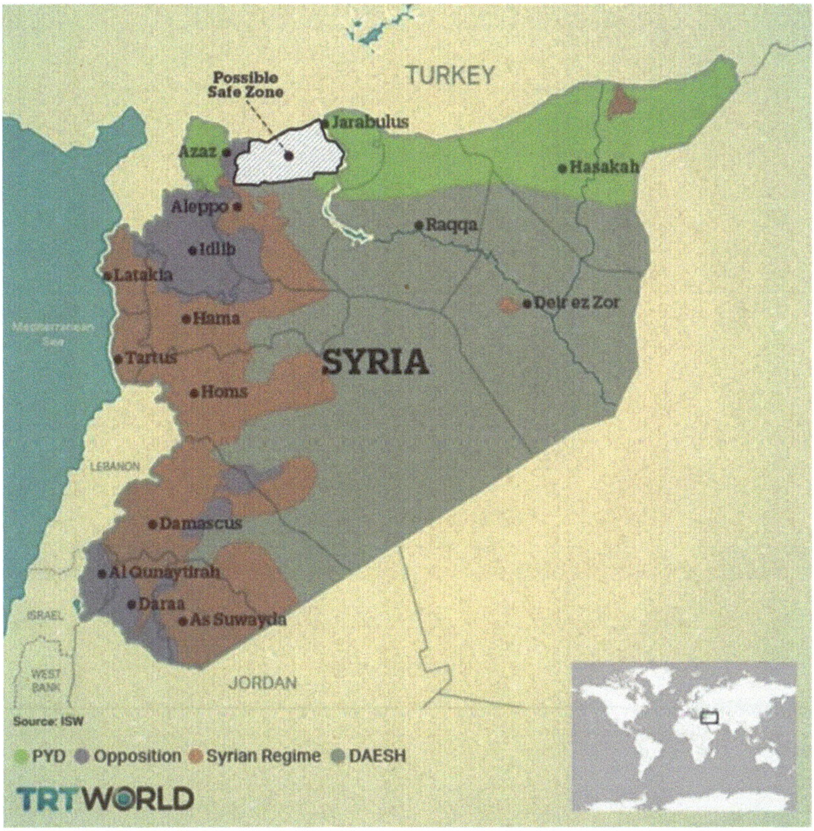

Fig. 3.3 Possible safe zone in Syria proposed by Turkey. *Source* Murat Sofuoglu, 'Safe zone' calls for Syrian refugees in an unsafe country,' *TRTWORLD*, 25 April 2016 available at: http://www.trtworld.com/in-depth/safe-zone-calls-for-syrian-refugees-in-an-unsafe-country-93759 [accessed: 5 September 2016]

This is due to Turkey's national security concerns as its Syrian border is at risk of being wholly controlled by PKK/PYD/YPG. Military operations that began on 24 August 2016 have ensured that DAESH presently controls no land along the Turkish border in Syria (Figs. 3.4 and 3.5).

Establishment of such a zone between the northern Syrian towns of Azaz and Jarablus would address the following three problems. First, it may obstruct connection of Kurdish cantons on the ground by keeping Kurdish PYD/YPG, which is the Syrian branch of Turkey's own Kurdish insurgents PKK, in the east of Euphrates River. This is important for Syria's territorial integrity by not allowing a

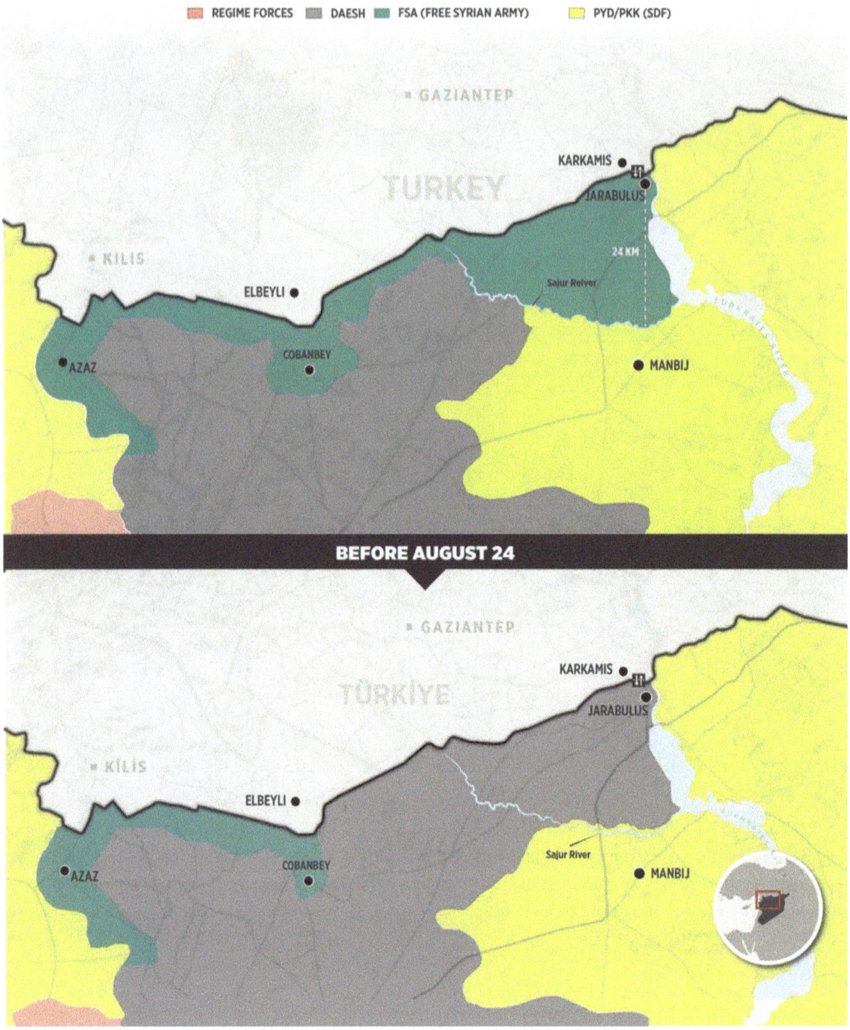

Fig. 3.4 Turkish border with Syria before Operation Euphrates Shield started on 24 August 2016 and the situation twelve days after the operation. *Source* 'Turkish border with Syria cleared of Daesh terrorists,' *Anadolu Agency*, 4 September 2016, available at: http://aa.com.tr/en/info/infographic/1871 [accessed: 10 September 2016]

separate Kurdish entity in northern Syria. Second, it may serve to keep DAESH at bay from Turkish border in Syria. The last but not the least, it may substantially reduce outflow of refugees by eliminating the need for flight, and even may enable Turkey and other countries to settle refugees who presently stay in their countries in

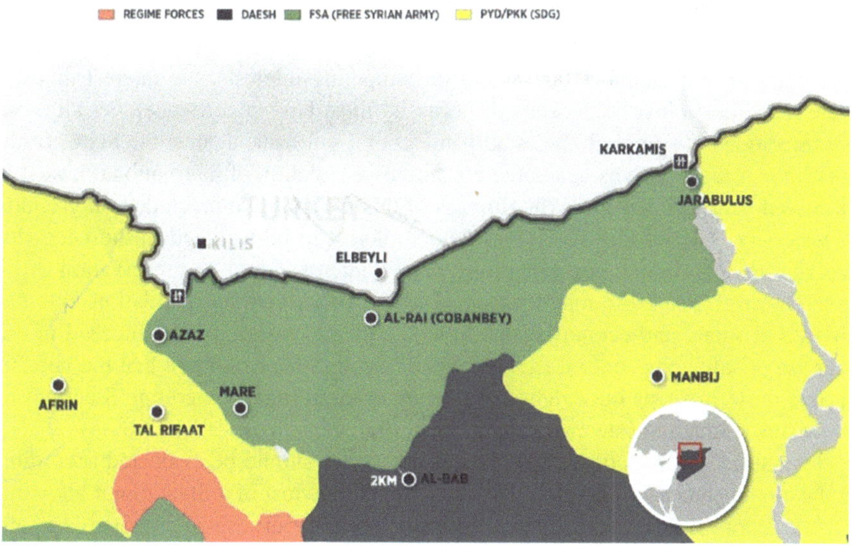

Fig. 3.5 Turkish-backed Free Syrian Army-held area near Turkish border in Syria as of 13 November 2016. *Source* 'FSA launches new phase to liberate Syria's Al-Bab,' *Anadolu Agency*, 13 November 2016, available at: http://aa.com.tr/en/info/infographic/2504 [accessed: 13 November 2016]

that zone. After the start of Turkey-backed Operation Euphrates Shield into northern Syria, some thousands of Syrian refugees have already returned to their own country from Turkey, which is reconnecting electricity and providing humanitarian aid to Jarablus in order to return life to normal in that area.[55]

Since an area cannot be made safe merely by international declaration, States must first evaluate the feasibility of the establishment of safe zones from the military point of view in order to not create a tragedy similar Bosnia. Second, political, monetary, and human costs of taking such measures must be well calculated to ensure effective initiation and maintenance of implementation.

Those previously analyzed options may be considered as an alternative to a refugee-receiving State under certain circumstances, but not for Turkey since it would be infeasible and unsuitable for it to cope with the ever-growing number of Syrian refugees. Therefore, there has not been a feasible alternative proposed to or by Turkey, irrespective of cost, to prevent the Syrian refugees from crossing its international border other than a safe zone, with the purpose to avert and even reverse such flows while ensuring the safety of refugees within their national homeland.

[55]Mark Lowen, 'Syria conflict: Life returns to Jarablus after IS flees' *BBC News*, 13 September 2016, available at: http://www.bbc.com/news/world-middle-east-37350970 [accessed: 14 September 2016].

3.1.4 Balancing Conflicting Interests

According to a reasonable assessment of competing interests, the interest that the State relied on to invoke the state of necessity must have precedence over all other considerations.[56] Although the establishment of a safe zone against the State within which the refugee flow is generated constitutes a violation of international law, it is discussed here whether the wrongfulness of this act could be precluded on grounds of necessity. The refugee-receiving State's interest to be weighed in the necessity analysis against the refugee-generating State's interest could be preservation of its sovereign rights and the maintenance of safety of its civilian population, internal order, and social and economic stability. The plea of necessity can succeed in the exercise of safe zones only if the refugee-receiving State can prove that the need to protect those interests outweighs the interest of the refugee-generating State not to allow other States to intervene on its territory.

The intrinsic values of the interests of both sides should be evaluated according to the circumstances of the case. For instance, the interest of a State in not allowing outside actors to intervene into its territory for the purpose of establishing safe zones would be of lesser importance by comparison with the interest of any other State in preservation of its sovereign rights. This is the case in Syria where the Assad government has already lost its control over significant parts of its territory to DAESH, Kurdish militias, and opposition forces for a significant period of time (Fig. 3.6).

Whereas the Syrian government is unable to control even a square meter alongside its 911 km border with Turkey, how can Turkey be expected to strictly respect the sovereignty of Syria while its sovereign right to determine who is allowed to enter its territory has been violated for the past half decade? Hence, in view of the situation of Syria, the Assad government has to tolerate intervention by outside powers so long it is unable to prevent trans-border security threats originating from its territory. In light of the aforementioned facts, the interest of Syria not to allow other States to intervene on its territory would be of lesser value than the necessity to safeguard Turkey's interest, namely the preservation of its sovereign right to determine who is allowed to enter its territory and the maintenance of safety of its civilian population, internal order, and social and economic stability.

As safe zones are created to halt refugee flows and provide safety to displaced persons within their country of origin, such establishments should not be assessed like other intervention[s] intended to overthrow a government or annex a part of its territory. It is important to note that Turkey has long laid emphasis on Syria's territorial integrity as a top priority in its Syria policy.[57] In this respect, it is the least

---

[56] ARSIWA Commentary, Art 25, para 17.

[57] 'Turkish army in Syria in response to continuous terrorist attacks, President Erdogan says' *Daily Sabah*, 24 August 2016, available at: http://www.dailysabah.com/war-on-terror/2016/08/24/turkish-army-in-syria-in-response-to-continuous-terrorist-attacks-president-erdogan-says [accessed: 4 September 2016].

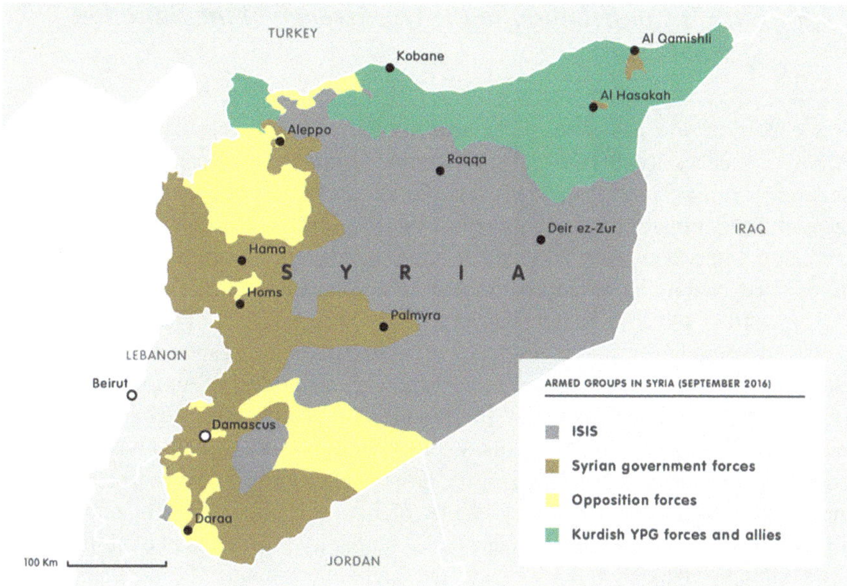

Fig. 3.6 Armed groups in Syria as of September 2016. *Source* Jihad Yazigi, 'No Going Back: Why Decentralisation is the Future for Syria,' European Council On Foreign Relations, September 2016, at 5, available at: http://www.ecfr.eu/page/-/ECFR185_-_NO_GOING_BACK_-_WHY_DECENTRALISATION_IS_THE_FUTURE_FOR_SYRIA.pdf [accessed: 9 September 2016]

intrusive way to intervene in another country. On the other hand, such distinctions may threaten legal stability by paving the way for interventions of various purposes in the name of humanitarian concerns. However, no State may be obliged to continuously suffer from an ever-growing refugee influx tied to social, political, economic, and security risks, emanating from an unstable neighbor in order to respect the refuge-generating State's territorial sovereignty. This is due to the fact that a country that creates conditions that compel persons on its territory to leave internationalizes what might otherwise be regarded purely as an internal matter.[58] Although territorial sovereignty is still regarded as a cornerstone of public international law, this principle should not be a shield for governments to continuously and consciously disregard its international obligations.

In conclusion, the interest of Turkey in the establishment of a safe zone in Syria prevails over Syrian interests. This is due to the fact that Turkey aims to preserve its sovereign rights and maintain a stable and secure environment for its civilian population while Syria has not even had control for the past half decade of a part of its territory from where Syrian refugees emanate.

---

[58]Gil Loescher, *supra* note 20, at 32; Myron Weiner, *supra* note 22, at 125.

3.1.5 State's Contribution to the Occurrence of the Situation of Necessity

This condition was also one of the reasons why the ICJ rejected the Hungary's defense of necessity in the case concerning *Gabčíkovo–Nagymaros Project.*[59] Accordingly, if a State substantially contributed to the occurrence of the situation of necessity intentionally or by negligence, the ICJ does not accept that State's reliance on the necessity plea.[60] However, mere incidental or peripheral contributions are deemed insufficient to deprive a State of the necessity plea.[61]

The conflict in Syria began with civilian protests in 2011. The Assad government's oppressive response by use of indiscriminate weapons, arbitrary and extensive detentions, torture and other types of mistreatment, and even chemical weapons[62] to those protests turned the situation into a civil war.[63] The Independent International Commission of Inquiry on the Syrian Arab Republic (IICISAR) indicated that both the Assad government and rebel groups have perpetrated systematic and widespread grave violations of human rights and humanitarian law amounting to war crimes and crimes against humanity.[64] Brutalities of conflicts and gross human rights violations create the breeding grounds for radical political movements and terrorism from which Syrian civilians flee.

By considering the relation map of Turkey with domestic actors in Syria, it would be correct to note that Turkey has no role in the conflicts between the Assad government, DAESH and Syrian Kurdish militias. Turkey has been principally opposed to Syrian Kurdish militias and DAESH, which pose a security risk to its territory, in order to keep them away from its borders. In order not to allow a separate entity or Kurdish corridor near the Turkish border, Turkey has also been supporting the Syrian opposition consisting of Syrian Turkmens and Arabs.[65] In addition, several States other than Turkey have also conducted military operations in Syria such as Australia, Bahrain, Canada, France, Jordan, the Netherlands, Saudi Arabia, Russia, UAE, UK, and US. In such a sophisticated case, one should not go too far in assessing Turkey's support to opposition groups as a substantial contribution to the occurrence of non-international armed conflict from which Syrian civilians flee.

---

[59] *Gabčíkovo-Nagymaros Project (Hungary v Slovakia),* ICJ Reports 1997, 7, para 57.

[60] *Idem*, para 52.

[61] ARSIWA Commentary, Art 25, para 20.

[62] UNHRC, 1st Report of the IICISAR, (2011) A/HRC/S-17/2/Add.1.

[63] UNHRC, 3rd Report of the IICISAR, (2012) A/HRC/21/50.

[64] UNHRC, 10th Report of the IICISAR, (2015) A/HRC/30/48.

[65] Tim Arango, Anne Barnard and Ceylan Yeginsu, 'Turkish-backed rebels drive IS from Syrian town Jarablus' *The Globe and Mail Online*, 24 August 2016, available at: http://www.theglobeandmail.com/news/world/turkey-starts-targeted-operations-against-islamic-state-syrian-fighters/article31528917/ [accessed 4 September 2016].

3.2 Application of the Necessity Doctrine to Justify Forcible Action Abroad

As the question whether the prohibition on use of force is of peremptory character has been discussed in detail in Sect. 2.3.1: 'Character of use of force,' debates and uncertainty over its asserted peremptory character will not be addressed in this section. However, it is important to note that there is no dispute as regard the customary character of the prohibition of the threat or use of force as codified in Article 2(4) of the Charter.[66] Despite the predominant view in international law doctrine that categorizes the prohibition on the use of force as a part of international *jus cogens*,[67] it is claimed here that this view does not reflect the current international law, an outcome of State practice. Therefore, the justification of establishing safe zones by the plea of necessity would not be in contradiction with Article 26 ARSIWA that excludes the possibility of relying on any circumstances listed under Chapter V to preclude the wrongfulness of an act that is not in conformity with an obligation arising under a peremptory norm.

According to the predominant view in international law doctrine, all uses of force are prohibited under *jus ad bellum* save for the two codified exceptions in the UN Charter. However, as has been indicated by Christakis,[68] limited military actions that clearly do not constitute aggression could be justified by a state of necessity if its requirements are met in a specific case. The possibility that certain acts implying use of force could be justified by necessity has been touched upon by the ILC in its 1980 Report: 'certain actions by States on the territory of other States which, although they may sometimes be of a coercive nature, serve only limited intentions and purposes bearing no relation to the purposes characteristic of a true act of aggression.'[69] Therefore, the very use of armed forces, under certain circumstances, may fall within the scope of justifiable use of force. For instance, some limited temporary interventions of military forces with the aim of establishing safe zones on foreign territory, with no real gravity, to forestall further influx of refugees by ensuring their safety within their country of origin where the territorial State has lost its control for a long time can be assessed within that scope.

The Commentary to Article 25 ARSIWA indicates that the state of necessity has been invoked to justify forcible action abroad in some cases such as in Belgium's

---

[66]International Law Association (ILA), Draft Report on Aggression and the Use of Force (Johannesburg Conference, May 2016), at 2.

[67]Albrecht Randelzhofer and Oliver Dörr, 'Article 2(4)', in: B. Simma et al. (eds), *The Charter of the United Nations: A Commentary* Vol. I (2nd edn, OUP, 2012) 200, at 231; Charles Leben, 'Obligations Relating to The Use of Force and Arising From Peremptory Norms of International Law', in: J. Crawford, A. Pellet and S. Olleson (eds), *The Law of International Responsibility* (New York: OUP, 2010) 1177, at 1202.

[68]Theodore Christakis, 'Intervention and Self-help', in: K. Bannelier, T. Christakis and S. Heathcote (eds), *The ICJ and the Evolution of International Law: the Enduring Impact of the "Corfu Channel" Case* (London: Routledge, 2012) 211, at 212.

[69]ILC Report, *supra* note 13, at 43 para 23.

military interventions both into the Congo in 1960 and 1964, and into Kosovo in 1999.[70] The UK also relied on state of necessity with respect to Kosovo in 1999 before the Security Council.[71] However, the ILC does not express a view as to whether such forcible intervention would be lawful under the rule in Article 25.[72]

Salmon lists the cases where necessity has been invoked in the past to justify 'annexations of Krakow by Austria in 1846; of Rome by Italy in 1870; of Bosnia-Herzegovina by Austria-Hungary in 1908; of Ethiopia by Italy in 1870; as well as the occupation of Belgium and Luxemburg in 1914 by Germany; of Korea by Japan during the Russian-Japanese war; of Denmark, Norway, the Netherlands, Belgium, and Luxemburg by Germany; and of Yugoslavia and Greece by Italy, during the Second World War.'[73] However, as Heathcote indicates,[74] the necessity plea has been abused in a number of those cases for purposes of achieving political power. In order for the plea of necessity not to serve such ulterior purposes in the name of protection of vital interests, exceptional character was attributed to it in the second half of the twentieth century.

Although it has been frequently referred to as an example of self-defense, the *Caroline* Incident of 1837 is in fact one of the very first examples of the plea of necessity.[75] As the *Caroline* was being used to aid the Canadian insurgents, the British government destroyed that vessel within the US territory by reason of the fact that British rebels had been allowed to use US territory in order to assist Canadian insurgents. The critical question here is whether employment of force for the purpose of defending its security on foreign territory would still be justifiable in the post-Charter age. Instead of seeking 'one blanket solution,' it would be more consistent with the nature of international law, an outcome of State practice, to consider whether a circumstance serves to preclude the wrongfulness of an action on a case-by-case basis.[76]

The plea of necessity appears in the international law system as a temporary exception that enables States to manage unforeseen crises. Since the issue of large-scale influx of refugees has started to be seen more frequently in the second half of the twentieth century and has not been addressed in treaty or customary law before, it perfectly fits to invoke necessity if its requirements are met. Therefore,

---

[70] *Legality of Use of Force (Serbia and Montenegro v Belgium)*, Oral Pleading of Mr. Ergec for Belgium, 10 May 1999, CR 99/15, at 7.

[71] Statement of the United Kingdom permanent representative to the Security Council, S/PV3988, 24 March 1999, at 12.

[72] ARSIWA Commentary, Art 25, para 21.

[73] J. J. A. Salmon, 'Faut-il codifier l'état de nécessité en droit international', in J. Makarczyk (ed), *Essays in Honour of Judge Manfred Lachs* (Martinus Nijhoff, 1984) 235, at 243, cited in Sarah Heathcote, *supra* note 16, at 492.

[74] Sarah Heathcote, *supra* note 16, at 492.

[75] Louise Arimatsu, 'The Law of State Responsibility in Relation to Border Crossings: An Ignored Legal Paradigm', 89 *International Law Studies* 21 (2013), at 41.

[76] Vaughan Lowe, 'Precluding Wrongfulness or Responsibility: A Plea for Excuses', 10 *European Journal of International Law* 405 (1999), at 411.

Turkey may have invoked the plea of necessity as an excuse for its proposal for the establishment of a safe zone in Syria, much as Tanzania relied on this defense for its border closure policy in 1995 after welcoming 500,000 Rwandan refugees in 1994.

Turkey is already home to almost three million Syrian refugees, making it the host country with the largest refugee population in the world.[77] However, it is not only the number that differs between Turkey and other States, but also the extraordinarily destructive effects of the large-scale influx of Syrian refugees on the country's preservation of its sovereign rights and the maintenance of safety of its civilian population, internal order, and social and economic stability. The uniqueness of the situation that Turkey encounters in Syria where the Assad government has been unable and unwilling to halt the large-scale outflow of refugees yet and has been unwilling to consent to intervention of Turkey to do so, entitles Turkey to resort to the degree and kind of force that is necessary to ensure the cessation of such outflow. Establishment of safe zones, which appears to be the only means by which Turkey can safeguard its essential interests under the circumstances at hand, would be the most appropriate way to achieve that goal. Hence, had Turkey taken the measure of establishment of safe zones in Syria in the absence of any other possible appropriate response to the large-scale influx of Syrian refugees, its wrongfulness would have been precluded under the customary international law plea of necessity.

One must also bear in mind that Article 25 ARSIWA is formulated in a way that allows unilateral action, but may also contain collective action with other States or international organizations.[78] Therefore, it is also conceivable that a coalition of States or international organizations such as NATO might address the issue of large-scale refugee outflow—something not foreseen by the law at the time that Turkey's proposal for a safe zone in Syria was discussed.

---

[77]European Commission Humanitarian Aid and Civil Protection, *Turkey: Refugee Crisis*, September 2016, at 1, available at: http://ec.europa.eu/echo/files/aid/countries/factsheets/turkey_syrian_crisis_en.pdf [accessed: 9 September 2016].

[78]ARSIWA Commentary, Art 25, para. 15.

Chapter 4
Application of the Humanitarian Intervention Doctrine to Justify the Establishment of Safe Zones to Alleviate Human Suffering

The term 'humanitarian intervention' may be defined as a 'forceful intervention for humanitarian purposes by a third State or States to save the people of a State from their own Government's action or inaction.'[1] Adelman indicates that the establishment of safe zones, as a form of military action, may well be considered within the scope of humanitarian intervention since such zones would not only serve to prevent refugees from crossing an international border, but also ensure security to those at risk within their national homeland.[2]

It is widely accepted today that the Security Council has the authority, under Chapter VII of the UN Charter, to adopt or authorize humanitarian intervention into countries where conflicts remaining within a single State's boundary are causing severe humanitarian suffering. In the face of clear and significant humanitarian crises remaining within a single State's boundary, the Security Council has authorized military measures on multiple occasions such as in Bosnia and Herzegovina (1992),[3] Somalia (1992),[4] Rwanda (1993–4),[5] Haiti (1994),[6] and East Timor (1999),[7] and more recently in Libya (2011).[8] However, the Security Council has been deadlocked on Syria due to opposition from Russia and China—two veto-wielding permanent member States—to any international military measure.[9]

---

[1]International Law Association (ILA), Draft Report on Aggression and the Use of Force (Johannesburg Conference, May 2016) at 15.
[2]Howard Adelman, 'The Ethics of Humanitarian Intervention: The Case of the Kurdish Refugees', 6(1) *Public Affairs Quarterly* 61 (1992), at 62.
[3]SC Res 770, 12 August 1992, op para 2; SC Res 776, 14 September 1992, op para 2.
[4]SC Res 794, 3 December 1992, preamble and op para 10.
[5]SC Res 872, 5 October 1993, op paras 2, 3; SC Res 929, 22 June 1994, op para 3.
[6]SC Res 940, 31 July 1994, op para 4.
[7]SC Res 1264, 15 September 1999, op para 3.
[8]SC Res 1973, 17 March 2011, op para 4.
[9]'Speakers Call for Voluntary Suspension of Veto Rights in Cases of Mass Atrocity Crimes, as Security Council Debates Working Methods,' *Security Council 7052nd Meeting*, 29 October 2013, available at http://www.un.org/press/en/2013/sc11164.doc.htm [accessed: 12 July 2016].

L.B. Çetinkaya, *Safe Zone*, SpringerBriefs in Law,
DOI 10.1007/978-3-319-51997-5_4

This section aims to address the question of whether it is legally permissible for ad hoc coalitions of States or an individual State to adopt forcible measures to protect civilians in cases where the Security Council is deadlocked by the exercise of veto power and lacks permission by the government of a target State. In particular, this section focuses on cases where the target State abuses its authority by committing gross and systematic human rights violations triggering a large-scale refugee outflow. Additionally this section explores whether and under what circumstances outside intervention by the establishment of safe zones may be justified under the concept of humanitarian intervention.

4.1 Responsibility to Protect or Humanitarian Intervention?

The report of the International Commission on Intervention and State Sovereignty (ICISS) on the responsibility to protect (R2P)[10] was embraced in Articles 138, 139 of the 2005 World Summit Outcome Document (WSOD) which was endorsed by the UN General Assembly in 2005[11] and reaffirmed by the UN Security Council in 2006.[12] However, as Nanda[13] and Bellamy[14] indicate, the concept of R2P in the WSOD differs from the formulation of the ICISS's proposal in some points. For instance, while the ICISS's proposal left the door open for restraints on the use of vetoes by permanent members of the UN Security Council in certain circumstances,[15] there is no mention of any limit on veto power in the WSOD. Another example is that while the ICISS's proposal included alternative means to activate the use of coercive measures,[16] no alternative was embraced in the WSOD. Such differences demonstrate the fact that we have two different formulations of R2P, even if their names remain same. However, what the international community understands by the concept of R2P is the formulation of the WSOD.

Although the concept of R2P appeared quite promising in the first decade of the twenty-first century, its abuse in Libya to topple President Gaddafi in 2011 undermined the credibility of the concept of R2P and shattered the hope for a widely embraced legal framework to provide grounds for military interventions into

[10]International Commission on Intervention and State Sovereignty (ICISS), *The Responsibility to Protect* (Ottawa: International Development Research Centre, 2001).

[11]GA Res 60/1, 24 October 2005, Arts 138, 139.

[12]SC Res 1674, 28 April 2006, op para 4.

[13]Ved P. Nanda 'The Future Under International Law of the Responsibility to Protect after Libya and Syria', 21(1) *Michigan State International Law Review* 1 (2013), at 8.

[14]Alex Bellamy, 'The Responsibility to Protect and the problem of military intervention', 84(4) *The Royal Institute of International Affairs* 615 (2008), at 623.

[15]ICISS, *supra* note 10, at XIII.

[16]*Idem*, at 53–55.

States that abuse their authority by committing gross and systematic violations of the basic human rights of their people. One may still argue that the R2P doctrine could be used to authorize military intervention to deal with forced population displacements in Syria. However, both Russia and China have threatened to veto any resolution calling for military action against Syria.[17] Therefore, Syrian civilians find themselves obligated to pay the price for abuse of the R2P doctrine in Libya in 2011.

As there is no serious contestation to the Security Council's powers under Chapter VII within the context of authorization of military intervention to deal with large-scale refugee movements, the R2P doctrine is nothing more than recognition of the Security Council's powers. Therefore, it is political rather than legal in character and remains little more than a slogan.[18] However, as Koh indicates in his articles,[19] there is a strong need to develop a new legal framework for humanitarian intervention in order to give due respect to both territorial sovereignty and prevention of deliberate gross violations of human rights in today's world of internal warfare.

Since the question of whether unilateral armed humanitarian intervention into a State that has abused its authority by gross and systematic violations of the basic human rights of its population is a legal use of force was left open even in the ICISS's report, arguments over the legality of unilateral armed humanitarian intervention fall outside the R2P framework.[20]

4.2 Breaking the Sovereignty Shield

There is no disputing the fact that sovereignty is a cornerstone of the international political and legal system. The UN Charter's prohibition on the use of force (Article 2(4)) and the related principle of non-intervention (Article 2(7)) constrain States from intervening in a country for humanitarian concerns. However, the principle of

[17]e.g., Louis Charbonneau and Michelle Nichols, 'U.N. Security Council Powers Meet Again on Syria; No Outcome' *Reuters*, 29 August 2013, available at http://www.reuters.com/article/2013/08/29/us-syria-crisis-un-idUSBRE97S17R20130829 [accessed: 5 July 2016].

[18]Aidan Hehir, 'The Responsibility to Protect: 'Sound and Fury Signifying Nothing'?', 24(2) *International Relations* 218 (2010), at 233.

[19]Harold Hongju Koh, 'Syria and the Law of Humanitarian Intervention (Part I: Political Miscues and U.S. Law)' *Just Security*, 26 September 2013, available at https://www.justsecurity.org/1158/koh-syria/ [accessed: 12 July 2016]; Harold Hongju Koh, 'Syria and the Law of Humanitarian Intervention (Part II: International Law and the Way Forward)' *Just Security*, 2 October 2013, available at https://www.justsecurity.org/1506/koh-syria-part2/ [accessed: 12 July 2016]; Harold Hongju Koh, 'Syria and the Law of Humanitarian Intervention (Part III—A Reply)' *Just Security*, 10 October 2013, available at https://www.justsecurity.org/1863/syria-law-humanitarian-intervention-part-iii-reply/ [accessed: 12 July 2016].

[20]Major Jeremy A. Haugh, 'Beyond R2P: A Proposed Test For Legalizing Unilateral Armed Humanitarian Intervention', 221 *Military Law Review* 1 (2014), at 21.

sovereignty also imposes on the State responsibilities toward those living in its territory.[21] If the territorial State fails in its mission, ICJ noted in the *Barcelona Traction* case,[22] then all States have a legal interest in the protection of the basic rights of the human person, and any other State can act in its stead, even against its will.

Traditional conceptions of sovereignty have been challenged because of both humanitarian concerns and refugee flows across borders.[23] As Weiner rightly indicates, if a State creates conditions that compel its people to violate the boundaries of a neighboring country, then that State should expect others to intervene in its country to avert outflow of refugees.[24] Therefore, one should not fail to notice the relationship between sovereignty and the responsibility of the State for both the safety of its people and the protection of other States' rights within its territory.[25]

When the domestic acts and policies of a State result in gross and systematic human rights violations from which civilians flee across international borders, that State is violating its international obligations. This internationalizes what might otherwise be regarded purely as an internal matter. According to Lee,[26] individual and collective responses to these internationalized affairs of a refugee-generating State would not, under the circumstances, constitute an intervention in the internal affairs of the State.

Past examples of safe zone establishments constitute a clear indication that the consent of the country of origin of refugees may not be required under certain circumstances with reference to the strong need to address humanitarian suffering as well as overwhelming flows of refugees. Furthermore, it would be absurd to ask for the consent of the concerned authority that engages in activities amounting to war crimes and crimes against humanity, i.e., the Assad government, to provide security to the persons who are fleeing in response.

This 'sovereignty shield' has been broken since the end of the Cold War due to the fact that the Security Council has become more active in the authorization of the use of military force to alleviate humanitarian suffering that often creates refugee

---

[21]ICISS, *supra* note 10, at 13.

[22]*Barcelona Traction, Light and Power Company, Limited (Belgium v Spain),* Second Phase, Judgment, ICJ Reports 1970, 3, paras 33–34.

[23]Myron Weiner and Münz Rainer, 'Migrants, refugees and foreign policy: prevention and intervention strategies', 18(1) *Third World Quarterly* 25 (1997), at 27.

[24]Myron Weiner, 'Security, Stability, and International Migration', 17(3) *International Security* 91 (1992–3), at 126.

[25]Frank X. Njenga, 'The Establishment of Safety Zones for Displaced Persons in Their Country of Origin', in N. Al-Nauimi, R. Meese (eds), *International Legal Issues Arising Under the United Nations Decade of International Law* (The Netherlands: Martinus Nijhoff Publishers, 1995) 819, at 821.

[26]Luke T. Lee, 'Toward a World without Refugees: The United Nations Group of Governmental Experts on International Co-operation to Avert New Flows of Refugees', 57 *The British Yearbook of International Law* 317 (1986), at 332.

outflows. State practice has also developed in the same direction. Therefore, States may establish and militarily protect safe zones in order to preserve their interests as well as alleviate human suffering in today's world of internal warfare. Therefore, the proposal to establish safe zone in northern Syria should not be understood as intervention in the classical sense, since the aim is not to topple the Assad government, but rather to keep those who are in need of safety in militarily protected zones within their national homeland.

4.3 The Link Between Human Suffering, Refugee Outflows and International Security

States and international bodies have increasingly cited certain domestic acts and policies, especially those triggering large-scale influx of refugees, as a threat to international peace and security. This is especially the case when such policies pose a threat to the security of neighboring countries that are in turn obligated to incur the cost of those acts and policies by having refugees forced upon them *en masse*. The report of the UN Secretary-General indicated that conflicts remaining within a single State's boundary and causing severe humanitarian suffering by initiating large-scale outflow of refugees may constitute threats to international peace and security as well.[27] The close relationship between such violations, forced displacement, and regional security and stability provides grounds for justification of international military action, including forcible intervention into other countries.[28]

The UN Security Council has considered actual or anticipated large-scale outflow of refugees toward and across international borders a threat to international peace and security on many occasions.[29] Since the end of the Cold War, forced population displacement which threatens international peace and security has been the grounds for international military action, e.g., Liberia (1990), Iraq (1991), Somalia (1992–3), Bosnia and Herzegovina (1992–5), Rwanda (1993–4), Haiti (1994), Kosovo (1998–9), and Sierra Leone (1999–2000).[30] Those examples demonstrate the developing practice of using military action to protect displaced populations in their countries of origin.

---

[27]Boutros Boutros-Ghali, *Report on the Work of the Organization from the Forty-seventh to Forty-eighth Session of the General Assembly* (New York: United Nations, 1993) at 165.

[28]Gil Loescher, 'Refugees as Grounds for International Action', in E. Newman and J. van Selm (eds) *Refugee and forced displacement: International security, human vulnerability, and the state* (Tokyo: UNU Press, 2003) 31, at 42; Adam Roberts, 'Refugees and Military Intervention,' in A. Betts and G. Loescher (eds), *Refugees in International Relations* (New York: OUP, 2011) 213, at 213.

[29]See, inter alia, SC Res 688, 5 April 1991 op para 1; SC Res 794, 3 December 1992, preamble.

[30]Guy S. Goodwin-Gill, 'Editorial: Refugees and Security', 11(1) *International Journal of Refugee Law* 1 (1999), at 3; Gil Loescher, *supra* note 28, at 39–40; Adam Roberts, *supra* note 28, at 229.

For instance, as the military regime in Haiti triggered large-scale displacements of the Haitian population, the Security Council authorized the US's military intervention into Haiti under Chapter VII of the UN Charter by drawing attention to the burden of large-scale refugee influx on other States in that region constituting a threat to international peace and security.[31] Therefore, such outflows are grounds for invoking Chapter VII of the UN Charter and enforcement actions to avert such flows would not be subject to the limits of purely humanitarian action. Adelman says that this situation justifies defensive military intervention.[32]

The UN General Assembly established a seventeen-member group of governmental experts in 1981 to study refugee issues.[33] The group was then enlarged to twenty-five experts[34] from both refugee-generating and refugee-receiving countries. Therefore, disparate interests of both sides were at the table. To prevent the impression of bias against refugee-generating countries and to incentivize universal compliance with the conclusions and recommendations of the group, one-third of the group (eight out of a total of twenty-four regular members) was made up of refugee-generating countries, obviously a higher ratio than the proportion of all refugee-generating countries amongst the total number of UN member countries. The group succeeded in arriving at a consensus, and therefore contributed to progressive development of international law through its report on international co-operation to avert new flows of refugees, empowered by the General Assembly (Article 13(I)(a) of the UN Charter).[35] The conclusions and recommendations of the report, which reflect the consensus amongst group members since the group conducted itself bound by a unanimity rule, were endorsed by the General Assembly by consensus in 1986.[36]

The *Report on International Co-operation to Avert New Flows of Refugees* concludes that the emergence of large-scale flows of refugees carries adverse consequences for refugee-receiving States and endangers international peace and security.[37] Although dealing with large-scale flows of refugees is the responsibility of the States directly concerned in the first instance, this problem is also a matter of serious concern to the international community as a whole. The report obligates States to 'refrain from creating or contributing by their policies to causes and factors

---

[31]SC Res 940, 31 July 1994, preamble.

[32]Howard Adelman, *supra* note 2, at 75.

[33]GA Res 36/148, 16 December 1981.

[34]GA Res 37/121, 16 December 1982.

The group members were appointed by the Secretary-General, one each was nominated by Afghanistan, Australia, Austria, Bulgaria, Cuba, Czechoslovakia, Djibouti, Ethiopia, France, the Federal Republic of Germany, Honduras, Japan, Lebanon, Mexico, Nicaragua, Pakistan, Philippines, Senegal, Somalia, Sudan, Thailand, Togo, the USSR, the US and Vietnam. The twenty-fifth seat was rotated among the Latin-American, African and Asian regions.

[35]GA Res 41/324, 13 May 1986.

[36]GA Res 41/70, 3 December 1986.

[37]GA Res 41/324, 13 May 1986, para 63.

which generally lead to large-scale flows of refugees.'[38] It is also expected that States, individually and collectively, 'make provisions and take appropriate measures to avert new flows of refugees.'[39]

4.4 Historical Instances of Humanitarian Intervention

Frequently cited historical instances of military actions without Security Council authorization in the name of humanitarian intervention during and after the Cold War are briefly outlined here to survey State practice in this context.

As a result of the brutal policy of the new elected government of West Pakistan against the Bengali population of East Pakistan, an estimated eight million refugees poured into India in 1970–71.[40] In response, India intervened in East Pakistan in 1971 in support of the movement for an independent Bangladesh, and within months India sent the refugees home.[41] Similarly, after Vietnam-backed opposition forces in Cambodia failed to overthrow the Khmer Rouge government, which had committed widespread atrocities and engaged in border clashes, Vietnam intervened in Cambodia in 1978.[42] In addition, Tanzania intervened in Uganda in 1979 in response to the Ugandan Army's cross-border military actions. In the end, some Ugandan territory was occupied by Tanzania and the Idi Amin government, which perpetrated massive atrocities, was toppled.[43] The last example from the Cold War era is that France launched military operation in the Central African Republic in 1979 for former president, David Dacko, to retake power from Jean-Bedel Bokassa, who had committed gross human rights violations.[44]

It is true that these interventions during the Cold War prevented widespread massacres, further flights, and even enabled refugees to return home, but in the meantime the targeted regimes were toppled. Therefore, they were widely condemned as violations of national sovereignty.[45] Furthermore, Tanzania and Vietnam did not even explicitly rely on humanitarian arguments for their

[38]GA Res 41/324,13 May 1986, para 66(c).

[39]GA Res 41/324, 13 May 1986 para 66(g).

[40]Thomas M. Franck, *Recourse To Force: State Action Against Threats And Armed Attacks* (Cambridge: CUP, 2002) at 139–40.

[41]Myron Weiner, *supra* note 24, at 123.

[42]Nicholas J. Wheeler, *Saving Strangers: Humanitarian Intervention in International Society* (Oxford: OUP, 2002), at 79–82.

[43]*Idem*, at 111–114.

[44]Oona A. Hathaway, Tomas, VIctor, Brower and Liss, 'Consent-Based Humanitarian Intervention: Giving Sovereign Responsibility Back to the Sovereign', 46 *Cornell International Law Journal* 499 (2013), at 514–515.

[45]Alan Dowty and Gil Loescher, 'Refugee Flows as Grounds for International Action', 21/1 *International Security* 43 (1996), at 62.

interventions.[46] Therefore, it is important to note the difference between intervening with the purpose of establishing safe zones to alleviate human suffering and interventions that also topple the targeted regimes. Hence, establishment of a safe zone to ensure security to persons who flee conflict and violence is clearly not a means to intervene in the internal affairs of another State, unlike these historical examples of humanitarian intervention.

A use of force against repressive governments with the aim of saving prospective victims of gross and systematic human rights violations was widely accepted as a violation of the UN Charter during Cold War. However, this perception began to change during the post-Cold War era of the 1990s.

Economic Community of West African States (ECOWAS) dispatched its Cease-Fire Monitoring Group (ECOMOG), consisting of the armed forces of its member States, to intervene in Liberia (1990) and Sierra Leone (1997–1999). The reason for the intervention into Liberia was to ensure lasting ceasefire between the parties of the civil war, but no UN Security Council authorization existed for this.[47] Although ECOWAS was authorized by the Security Council only to ensure the implementation of the embargo in Sierra Leone,[48] ECOMOG adopted forcible measures and overthrew the military government.[49] These two instances are examples of regional humanitarian intervention.

Although there was a lack of explicit authorization by the UN Security Council or consent of the Iraqi government for military intervention of outside powers into its country, the UN Security Council's Resolution 688[50] was used by the US and its collation partners as a basis to establish safe zones in northern Iraq in 1992 for Kurds who were forced to leave their homes by the Iraqi government. Britain characterized its participation in the US-led intervention in Iraq as an 'exercise of the customary international law principle of humanitarian intervention.'[51] However, Resolution 688 did not contain a single word about the establishment of safe zones. It only allowed 'immediate access by international humanitarian organizations to all those in need of assistance in all parts of Iraq…' The resolution even made reference to the non-intervention principle (Art 2(7) of the UN Charter) that excludes any military intervention based on this resolution.

Resolution 688 considered that the large-scale flow of refugees toward and across international frontiers threatened international peace and security in the region.[52] Martin claims that the primary concern of Resolution 688 was Turkish

---

[46]Oona A. Hathaway, *supra* note 44, at 510.

[47]*Idem*, at 515.

[48]SC Res. 1132, 8 October, 1997, op para 8.

[49]UN Secretary-General, Fourth Report of the Secretary-General on the Situation in Sierra Leone, U.N. Doc. S/1998/249, (18 March 1998) para 6.

[50]SC Res 688, 5 April 1991.

[51]Nicholas J. Wheeler, *supra* note 42, at 215 (quoting the statement of a legal counselor to Britain's Foreign and Commonwealth Office).

[52]SC Res 688, 5 April 1991, preamble.

sensitivity toward the large-scale flow of Kurdish refugees rather than concern at their suffering.[53] Hutchinson says that it was a response to public pressure and was unjustifiably interpreted to allow the use of force to protect Kurds with safe zones.[54] The Western media and public put extreme pressure on political leaders to save Kurds using terrifying pictures and videos of the situation. Wheeler demonstrates the influential role the Western media played in taking the decision of establishment of safe zones in Iraq.[55] Since the operation was successful to save Kurds from that situation, other States abstained from criticizing it to avoid a media storm of condemnation. Wheeler considered the lack of criticism an indicator for setting a precedent similar action in future cases.[56] Laberge indicates that the silence of members of the Council that voted against (Cuba, Yemen, and Zimbabwe) or abstained from (China and India) Resolution 688 against establishment of safe zones in Iraq implies acknowledgment that customary international may develop 'by precedents of omission.'[57]

The last case after the Cold War which must be referred to here is NATO's intervention in Kosovo, where the fighting between the Federal Republic of Yugoslavia forces and the Kosovo Liberation Army resulted in forced displacement of at least 400,000 people and deaths of over 1,500 Kosovar Albanians.[58] Although the Security Council considered the situation in Kosovo a threat to international peace and security in Resolution 1199,[59] it could not adopt or authorize military measures due to opposition from two of the veto-wielding States, Russia and China.[60] The Independent International Commission on Kosovo considered NATO's military intervention 'illegal but legitimate,'[61] since it was the only available avenue left to save the population of Kosovo from Serbian oppression. This leads us to question if the overall protection of persons against gross and systematic violations of basic human rights, which is claimed to be a reflection of the spirit of the UN Charter, may render humanitarian intervention tolerable under international law even if it is inconsistent with the unambiguous formulation of UN

[53]David A. Martin, 'Strategies for a Resistant World: Human Rights Initiatives and the Need for Alternatives to Refugee Interdiction', 26 *Cornell International Law Journal* 753 (1993), at 765.

[54]Mark R. Hutchinson, 'Restoring Hope: UN Security Council Resolutions for Somalia and an expanded doctrine of Humanitarian Intervention', 34 *Harvard International Law Journal* 624 (1993), at 633.

[55]Nicholas J. Wheeler, *supra* note 42, at 167.

[56]*Idem*, at 154.

[57]Pierre Laberge, 'Humanitarian Intervention: Three Ethical Positions', 9 *Ethics and International Affairs* 15 (1995), at 31.

[58]Oona A. Hathaway, supra note 44, at 518.

[59]SC Res 1199, 23 September 1998, preamble.

[60]The Independent International Commission on Kosovo, *The Kosovo Report: Conflict, International Response, Lessons Learned* (New York: OUP, 2000) at 163.

[61]*Idem*, at 4.

Charter.[62] If unilateral humanitarian armed intervention in such situations is to be considered tolerable in international law, some concerns will be raised that '[t]he door will have been opened to all sorts of subjective claims as to when interventions are justified and when they are not.'[63] Therefore, if doubts of the legality of humanitarian intervention disappear in future, it must only be allowed under very strict and limited circumstances in order not to open the door for abuses.

4.5 Legality of Humanitarian Intervention and the Establishment of Safe Zones

Grewe surveys international law of past centuries to explore the origin and very first examples of humanitarian intervention.[64] Accordingly, although numerous humanitarian interventions occurred even in the nineteenth century, a normative framework for humanitarian intervention on a purely positivist basis had not yet been developed. Therefore, strict positivist lawyers widely opposed humanitarian intervention,[65] and some of them, such as Oppenheim,[66] deemed it valid only as a maxim of legal philosophy and policy. However, advocates of humanitarian intervention, mostly Anglo-Saxon international lawyers, argued that it was grounded in the law of humanity, which is claimed to be a binding part of international law.[67] Besides, Jennings referred to State practice and writings of scholars, as a subsidiary mean, in support of the legality of humanitarian intervention.[68]

Consistent and widespread State practice and *opinio juris* (States' performance of certain acts out of a sense of legal obligation) on humanitarian intervention needs to be clearly revealed in order to claim that it is of customary character. Loescher points out that the interventions of the 1990s set a precedent for international, regional, and unilateral armed humanitarian intervention in the internationalized affairs of States.[69] However, since the international community's position toward most of these interventions was not supportive, Sterio is of the opinion that although humanitarian intervention has not yet developed enough to be considered

[62]Milena Sterio, 'Humanitarian Intervention Post-Syria: Legitimate and Legal?', 40 *Brooklyn Journal of International Law* 109 (2014), at 125.

[63]Michael Byers, *Kosovo: An Illegal Operation* (Counsel, 1999), at 16–18.

[64]Wilhelm. G. Grewe, *The Ephocs of International Law*, (transl. and rev. by Michael Byers, Berlin; New York: de Gruyter, 2000), at 487–492.

[65]*Idem*, at 494.

[66]Lassa Oppenheim, *International Law*, 1905–06, at 137.

[67]Wilhelm. G. Grewe, *supra* note 64, at 493.

[68]Robert Y. Jennings, 'Some International Law Aspects of the Refugee Question', 20 *British Yearbook of International Law* 98 (1939), at 111.

[69]Gil Loescher, *supra* note 28, at 39.

a norm of customary law; it is an emerging norm that could develop into binding law in the near future.[70]

There are some scholars, such as Koh,[71] that claim the use of force within the scope of humanitarian intervention would not violate the UN Charter. However, such interpretations are widely rejected by reasoning that humanitarian concerns cannot take precedence over the ban on the use of force.[72] Those who disagree with Koh at least accept the fact that there is a growing need for the international community to be able to take actions through different mechanisms in cases where the Security Council is deadlocked because of the geo-political interests of its permanent veto-wielding members.[73] Some reports on Srebrenica and Rwanda, namely the *Report of the Secretary-General to the Security Council on the Protection of Civilians in Armed Conflict,*[74] *Report of the Secretary-General pursuant to General Assembly Resolution 53/35: The Fall of Srebrenica,*[75] and the *Report of the Independent Inquiry into the Actions of the United Nations during the 1994 Genocide in Rwanda,*[76] discuss how humanitarian and refugee issues may, and should, sometimes constitute a basis for the initiation of military action.

ILA, in the conclusion of its *Draft Report on Aggression and the Use of Force*, sheds light on the concerns of the international community at the failure to respond to humanitarian catastrophes, e.g., Rwanda, Darfur and Syria.[77] This is the primary reason why there is a growing need for a unilateral right to use force for humanitarian purposes as well as preventively when the Security Council is unwilling or unable to fulfill the role expected of it. A safe zone, as a form of military action, would be appropriate both for humanitarian purposes, by ensuring security to persons fleeing danger, and for prevention, by eliminating the need for flight across international borders.

Article 2(4) of the UN Charter's reference to 'armed' or 'physical' force[78] 'against the territorial integrity or political independence of any State' questions whether the resort to force for other purposes would still fall within the scope of the prohibition. As can be concluded from the *travaux* of the Charter,[79] the emphasis on territorial integrity and political independence was not intended to narrow the scope of the prohibition. Furthermore, Article 2(4) was formulated with broad terms in

[70]Milena Sterio, *supra* note 62, at 151.

[71]Harold Hongju Koh, *supra* note 19.

[72]David Kaye, 'Harold Koh's Case for Humanitarian Intervention' *Just Security*, 7 October 2013, available at https://www.justsecurity.org/1730/kaye-kohs-case/ [accessed: 12 July 2016].

[73]Milena Sterio, *supra* note 62, at 159.

[74]UN Doc. S/1999/957, 8 September 1999, at recommendation 40.

[75]UN Doc. A/54/549, published on 15 November 1999, at 102–107.

[76]UN Doc. S/1999/1257, 16 December 1999, at 54–57.

[77]ILA, *supra* note 1, at 19.

[78]Albrecht Randelzhofer and Oliver Dörr, 'Article 2(4)', in B. Simma et al. (eds) *The Charter of the United Nations: A Commentary* Vol. I (2nd edn, OUP, 2012) 200, at 209.

[79]Ian Brownlie, *International Law and the Use of Force by States* (Oxford: OUP, 1963), p. 267.

order not to leave loopholes, as evidenced by the phrase 'or in any other manner inconsistent with the Purposes of the United Nations.'[80]

If the aim for which the force is used matters in determination of the scope of the justifiable use of force, establishment of safe zones definitely constitutes an exception to the prohibition, since it serves to both protect the refugee-receiving State's interest by preventing outflow of refugees and to ensure the safety of individuals within their country of origin. However, considering military interventions for humanitarian purposes as an exception to the general prohibition of the use of force laid down in Article 2(4) of the UN Charter does not reflect the predominant view in international law.[81] It may be based more on considerations of pragmatism than of legality. However, it is worthwhile to analyze the Syria case within the context of humanitarian intervention in order to contribute to the international legal doctrine, which may eventually embrace such interpretation of present norms that allow establishment of safe zones in countries such as Syria.

According to the Syrian Observatory for Human Rights,[82] more than 300,000 people have been killed in the Syrian conflict since March 2011. More than 86,000 of that toll were civilians. According to Internal Displacement Monitoring Centre of the Norwegian Refugee Council,[83] more than 4.6 million Syrians have fled the country to seek refuge abroad and at least 6.6 million people were internally displaced inside Syria as of December 31, 2015. In the face of such an extraordinary humanitarian emergency, the international community has failed to persuade internal actors in Syria to put an end to gross and systematic human rights violations. As the conflict is ongoing with its brutality, a safe zone, as the least intrusive military measure available to States, seems the most acceptable solution to ensure security to persons at risk in Syria.

Since it has always been exceedingly difficult for States burdened by large-scale refugee outflows to persuade the international community to take measures necessary for alleviating human suffering and preventing refugee outflows, refugee-receiving States are often forced to take matters into their own hands. In this respect, it would seem that Turkey took the initiative by launching Operation Euphrates Shield on August 24, 2016 to clear the area proposed for a safe zone of terror groups. In the third week of the operation, some thousands of Syrian refugees have already returned to their own country from Turkey, which is reconnecting

[80]*United Nations Conference on International Organization Documents*, vol. 6 (San Francisco, 25 April 1945), at 334–335.

[81]Oona A. Hathaway, *supra* note 44, at 519.

[82]Syrian Observatory for Human Rights, 'About 430 thousands were killed since the beginning of the Syrian revolution', 13 September 2016, available at http://www.syriahr.com/en/?p=50612 [accessed: 14 September 2016].

[83]Internal Displacement Monitoring Centre (IDMC) of the Norwegian Refugee Council, 'Syria IDP Figures Analysis', available at http://www.internal-displacement.org/middle-east-and-north-africa/syria/figures-analysis [accessed: 14 September 2016].

electricity and providing humanitarian aid in order to return life to normal in that area.[84] If a safe zone can be established and maintained in a decisive manner, it may provide the safe return of refugees to their homeland as well as alleviate human suffering by providing security to persons at risk.

As safe zones differ from other forms of military intervention in the sense that such establishments carry no purpose of regime change or territorial adjustments, such establishments are likely to be regarded by the international community as an acceptable measure in the face of an extraordinary situation in Syria, unlike most of the historic examples in which targeted regimes were toppled. In this regard, intervening in Syria by establishing a safe zone temporarily to ensure security to civilians until security threats disappear would be the least intrusive way of dealing with humanitarian suffering in Syria and reducing the need for civilians to flee across international borders.

While the legal basis of humanitarian intervention is tenuous, some States such as the United Kingdom and Denmark have taken the position that humanitarian intervention could be a lawful option for Syria.[85]

4.6 Disinterest

Although 'disinterest' is often considered a necessary condition for humanitarian intervention,[86] Loescher argues that States acting not only on the basis of humanitarian grounds but also in their own interest to prevent refugee flows would make their actions even more effective and may eliminate the risk of experiencing tragedy similar to Bosnia.[87] However, the magnitude of humanitarian suffering still needs to be proved by the intervening State in order for its actions to fall under humanitarian intervention.

Sterio rightly indicates that where the self-defense paradigm is inapplicable, as in Syria, Rwanda, or Kosovo, the concept of humanitarian intervention would perfectly satisfy the need of States to take action for both protecting their interests and

[84]Mark Lowen, 'Syria conflict: Life returns to Jarablus after IS flees' *BBC News*, 13 September 2016, available at http://www.bbc.com/news/world-middle-east-37350970 [accessed: 14 September 2016].

[85]Harold Hongju Koh, 'Another Legal View of the Dissent Channel Cable on Syria' *Just Security*, 20 June 2016, available at https://www.justsecurity.org/31571/legal-view-dissent-channel-cable-syria/ [accessed: 4 September 2016].

[86]Harold Hongju Koh, 'Syria and the Law of Humanitarian Intervention (Part II: International Law and the Way Forward)' *Just Security*, 2 October 2013, available at https://www.justsecurity.org/1506/koh-syria-part2/ [accessed: 12 July 2016].

[87]Gil Loescher, *supra* note 28, at 39.

alleviating humanitarian suffering.[88] Therefore, 'disinterest' should not be considered as a condition *sine qua non*. Instead, if the interest of the State is also at stake, as in a case where the State wishes to prevent refugee outflows, it may even make the intervention more effective and successful since the motivation will be based on security grounds as well as humanitarian grounds.

[88]Milena Sterio, *supra* note 62, at 157.

Chapter 5
Conclusion

This work has examined the establishment of safe zones as a temporary military measure that ensures security for persons fleeing conflict and violence until such security threats disappear in their own country. The aim is not to intervene in a country's internal affairs, but to avert large-scale outflows of refugees. My analysis has suggested that safe zones can be an effective way to achieve the dual purpose of humanitarian protection and safeguarding of the interests of refugee-receiving States. Furthermore, I conclude that the concept of safe zone does not constitute an undue intervention into the internal affairs of the target State. When such a State internationalizes its internal affairs by initiating and failing to prevent large outflows of its people, safe zones may be justified on the grounds of countermeasures, necessity and humanitarian intervention.

As has been discussed under Chap. 2, it is possible to rely on State practice and interpret the relevant international law rules governing military actions abroad in a way that does not prevent a State from establishing safe zones on the territory of a refugee-generating country on the ground of countermeasures as long as its conditions are met. As the complete failure of the Syrian government in prevention of large-scale flows across international borders constitutes a breach of its international obligations and has had adverse consequences on the economic, political, and social stability, as well as the internal order and security of the community of Turkey, Syria must suffer the consequence of having Turkey, if decides to do so, establish safe zones within its territory until the need for such countermeasures disappears. In the absence of other means of redress, there is a high degree of legal acceptability that establishment of safe zones as a forcible countermeasure is a proportionate response to large-scale refugee outflows.

The plea of necessity, addressed under Chap. 3, appears in international law as a temporary exception that enables States to manage unforeseen crises. Since the issue of large-scale influx of refugees has been seen more frequently in the second half of the twentieth century, and has not been addressed in treaty or customary law before, it perfectly fits to invoke necessity if its requirements are met. The thesis argues that some limited temporary intervention of military forces with the aim of

L.B. Çetinkaya, *Safe Zone*, SpringerBriefs in Law,
DOI 10.1007/978-3-319-51997-5_5

establishing safe zones on foreign territory, with no real gravity and in areas where the territorial State has lost control for some time, in order to forestall further influx of refugees by ensuring their safety within their country of origin, can be justified by necessity.

The uniqueness of the situation that Turkey encounters in Syria where the Assad government has been unable and unwilling to halt the large-scale outflow of refugees and has been unwilling to consent to intervention by Turkey to do so, entitles Turkey to resort to the degree and kind of force that is necessary to ensure the cessation of such outflow. Establishment of safe zones, which appears as the only means by which Turkey can safeguard its essential interests under the circumstances at hand, would be the most appropriate way to achieve that goal. Hence, had Turkey taken the measure of establishment of safe zones in Syria in the absence of any other possible appropriate response to the large-scale influx of Syrian refugees, its wrongfulness would have been precluded under the customary international law plea of necessity.

Although humanitarian intervention, addressed under Chap. 4, is regarded as an emerging norm that could develop into binding law in the near future, it has not yet developed enough to be considered a norm of customary law. Therefore, the legal basis of humanitarian intervention remains tenuous. Nevertheless, if a State (or group of States) decides to establish and maintain safe zones in Syria in the name of humanitarian intervention, it may be found 'illegal but legitimate' once again. As safe zones differ from other forms of military intervention in the sense that such establishments carry no purpose of regime change or territorial adjustments, they are likely to be regarded by the international community as an acceptable measure in the face of the extraordinary situation in Syria, unlike most of the historic examples in which targeted regimes were toppled.

Beside the question of legality of establishment of safe zones, it must be noted here that this measure must be taken only when outside powers are willing and prepared to provide supplies and use military force when needed in the defense of safe zones in an effort to not repeat the tragedy of Bosnia. This is due to the fact that an area cannot be made safe merely by international declaration. States must evaluate the feasibility of safe zones on a case-by-case basis, and carefully calculate the political, monetary, and human costs of taking such measures to ensure their effective initiation, implementation and maintenance.

References

UN Materials

1. Boutros Boutros-Ghali, *Report on the Work of the Organization from the Forty-seventh to Forty-eighth Session of the General Assembly* (New York: United Nations, 1993).
2. GA Res 3314(XXIX), 14 December 1974.
3. GA Res 36/148, 16 December 1981.
4. GA Res 37/121, 16 December 1982.
5. GA Res 41/324, 13 May 1986.
6. GA Res 41/70, 3 December 1986.
7. GA Res 60/1, 24 October 2005.
8. Kofi A. Annan, *Preventing war and disaster: a growing global challenge—Annual Report on the Work of the Organization*, (New York: United Nations Department of Public Information, 1999).
9. *Report of the Secretary-General to the Security Council on the Protection of Civilians in Armed Conflict*, UN Doc. S/1999/957, 8 September 1999.
10. *Report of the Secretary-General pursuant to General Assembly Resolution 53/35: The Fall of Srebrenica* UN Doc. A/54/549, published on 15 November 1999.
11. *Report of the Independent Inquiry into the Actions of the United Nations during the 1994 Genocide in Rwanda,* UN Doc. S/1999/1257, 16 December 1999.
12. SC Res 688, 5 April 1991.
13. SC Res 770, 12 August 1992.
14. SC Res 776, 14 September 1992.
15. SC Res 794, 3 December 1992.
16. SC Res 819, 16 April 1993.
17. SC Res 824, 6 May 1993.
18. SC Res 836, 4 June 1993.
19. SC Res 844, 18 June 1993.
20. SC Res 859, 24 August 1993.
21. SC Res 872, 5 October 1993.
22. SC Res 918, 17 May 1994.
23. SC Res 925, 8 June 1994.
24. SC Res 929, 22 June 1994.
25. SC Res 940, 31 July 1994.
26. SC Res 1132, 8 October 1997.
27. SC Res 1199, 23 September 1998.
28. SC Res 1264, 15 September 1999.
29. SC Res 1674, 28 April 2006.
30. SC Res 1973, 17 March 2011.

L.B. Çetinkaya, *Safe Zone*, SpringerBriefs in Law,
DOI 10.1007/978-3-319-51997-5

31. Statement of the United Kingdom permanent representative to the Security Council, S/PV3988, 24 March 1999.
32. *United Nations Conference on International Organization Documents, vol. 6 (San Francisco, 25 April 1945).*
33. UN Secretary-General, *Fourth Report of the Secretary-General on the Situation in Sierra Leone*, U.N. Doc. S/1998/249, (18 March 1998).
34. UNHRC, *1st Report of the IICISAR*, (2011) A/HRC/S-17/2/Add.1.
35. UNHRC, *3rd Report of the IICISAR*, (2012) A/HRC/21/50.
36. UNHRC, *10th Report of the IICISAR*, (2015) A/HRC/30/48.

ILC Materials

37. Articles on the Responsibility of States for Internationally Wrongful Acts, II(2) *ILC Yearbook* 26 (2001).
38. Commentary to the Articles on the Responsibility of States for Internationally Wrongful Acts, II(2) *ILC Yearbook* 36 (2001).
39. ILC Report on the Work of its Thirty-Second Session, II(2) *ILC Yearbook* (1980).
40. *ILC Yearbook* 1995/II/2, 48th Session.
41. Roberto Ago, 'Addendum to the eighth report on State responsibility' II(1) *ILC Yearbook* 13 (1980).

Books

42. Adam Roberts, 'Refugees and Military Intervention', in A. Betts and G. Loescher (eds), *Refugees in International Relations* (New York: OUP, 2011) 213.
43. Agnes G. Hurwitz, *The Collective Responsibility of States to Protect Refugees* (USA: OUP, 2009).
44. Albrecht Randelzhofer & Oliver Dörr, 'Article 2(4)', in: B. Simma et al. (eds), *The Charter of the United Nations: A Commentary* Vol. I (2nd edn, OUP, 2012) 200.
45. Antonio Cassese, *International Law* (2nd edn, OUP, 2010).
46. B. S. Chimni, 'The Incarceration of Victims: Deconstructing Safety Zones', in: N. Al-Nauimi & R. Meese (eds), *International Legal Issues Arising Under the United Nations Decade of International Law* (The Netherlands: Martinus Nijhoff Publishers, 1995) 823.
47. Charles Leben, 'Obligations Relating to The Use of Force and Arising From Peremptory Norms of International Law', in: J. Crawford, A. Pellet & S. Olleson (eds), *The Law of International Responsibility* (New York: OUP, 2010) 1177.
48. David A. Martin 'Refugees and Migration', in: O. Schachter &. C. C. Joyner (eds), 1 *United Nations Legal Order* (CUP, 1995) 391.
49. Denis Alland, 'The Definition of Countermeasures', in: J. Crawford, A. Pellet & S. Olleson (eds), *The Law of International Responsibility* (New York: OUP, 2010) 1127.
50. Frank X. Njenga, 'The Establishment of Safety Zones for Displaced Persons in Their Country of Origin', in: N. Al-Nauimi, R. Meese (eds), *International Legal Issues Arising Under the United Nations Decade of International Law* (The Netherlands: Martinus Nijhoff Publishers, 1995) 819.
51. Gil Loescher, 'Refugees as Grounds for International Action', in: E. Newman & J. van Selm (eds), *Refugee and forced displacement: International security, human vulnerability, and the state* (Tokyo: UNU Press, 2003) 31.

52. Guy S. Goodwin-Gill, *The Refugee in International Law* (UK: OUP, 1983).
53. Guy S. Goodwin-Gill, *The Refugee in International Law* (2nd edn, New York: Clarendon Press, 1996).
54. Ian Brownlie, *International Law and the Use of Force by States* (Oxford: OUP, 1963).
55. Ian Brownlie, *Principles of Public International Law* (3rd edn, UK: OUP, 1979).
56. International Commission on Intervention and State Sovereignty (ICISS), *The Responsibility to Protect* (Ottawa: International Development Research Centre, 2001).
57. James A. Green, *The International Court of Justice and Self-Defence in International Law* (Oxford: Hart Publishing, 2009).
58. Jean-Philippe Lavoyer, 'International Humanitarian Law, Protected Zones and the Use of Force', in W. Biermann & M. Vadset (eds), *UN Peacekeeping in Trouble: Lessons Learned from the Former Yugoslavia* (Brookfield: Ashgate, 1998) 262.
59. Lassa Oppenheim, *International Law,* Vol. 1: Peace, H. Lauterpacht (ed) (8th edn, London: Longmans, Green, 1955).
60. Leon Gordenker, *Refugees in International Politics* (New York: Columbia University Press, 1987).
61. Linos-Alexandre Sicilianos 'Countermeasures in Response to Grave Violations of Obligations Owed to the International Community', in: J. Crawford, A. Pellet & S. Olleson (eds), *The Law of International Responsibility* (New York: OUP, 2010) 1137.
62. Maurice Kamto, 'The Time Factor in the Application of Countermeasures', in: J. Crawford, A. Pellet & S. Olleson (eds), *The Law of International Responsibility* (New York: OUP, 2010) 1169.
63. Michael Byers, *Kosovo: An Illegal Operation* (Counsel, 1999).
64. Myron Weiner (ed), *International Migration and Security* (Boulder, CO: Westview Press, 1993).
65. Nicholas J. Wheeler, *Saving Strangers: Humanitarian Intervention in International Society* (Oxford: OUP, 2002).
66. Roger O'Keefe, 'Proportionality', in: J. Crawford, A. Pellet & S. Olleson (eds), *The Law of International Responsibility* (New York: OUP, 2010) 1157.
67. Sarah Heathcote, 'Circumstances Precluding Wrongfulness in the ILC Articles on State Responsibility: Necessity', in: J. Crawford, A. Pellet & S. Olleson (eds), *The Law of International Responsibility* (New York: OUP, 2010) 491.
68. Sarah Heathcote, 'State Omissions and Due Diligence: Aspects of Fault, Damage and Contribution to Injury in the Law of State Responsibility', in: K. Bannelier, T. Christakis & S. Heathcote (eds), *The ICJ and the Evolution of International Law: The Enduring Impact of the Corfu Channel Case* (UK: Routledge, 2012) 295.
69. Stanley Hoffman, *Duties beyond Borders: On the Limits and Possibilities of Ethical International Politics* (New York: Syracuse University Press, 1981).
70. The Independent International Commission on Kosovo, *The Kosovo Report: Conflict, International Response, Lessons Learned* (New York: OUP, 2000).
71. Theodore Christakis, 'Intervention and Self-help', in: K. Bannelier, T. Christakis & S. Heathcote (eds), *The ICJ and the Evolution of International Law : the Enduring Impact of the "Corfu Channel" Case* (London: Routledge, 2012) 211.
72. Thomas M. Franck, *Recourse To Force: State Action Against Threats And Armed Attacks* (Cambridge: CUP, 2002).
73. Wilhelm. G. Grewe, *The Ephocs of International Law*, (transl. and rev. by Michael Byers, Berlin; New York: de Gruyter, 2000).
74. Yuji Iwasawa and Naoki Iwatsuki, 'Procedureal Conditions', in: J. Crawford, A. Pellet & S. Olleson (eds) *The Law of International Responsibility* (New York: OUP, 2010) 1149.

Academic Journal Articles

75. Aidan Hehir, 'The Responsibility to Protect: 'Sound and Fury Signifying Nothing'?', 24(2) *International Relations* 218 (2010).
76. Alan Dowty & Gil Loescher, 'Refugee Flows as Grounds for International Action', 21/1 *International Security* 43 (1996).
77. Alex Bellamy, 'The Responsibility to Protect and the problem of military intervention', 84 (4) *The Royal Institute of International Affairs* 615 (2008).
78. Augustine Mahiga, 'A Change of Direction for Tanzania', 110 *Refugees Magazine* 14 (1997).
79. David A. Martin, 'Strategies for a Resistant World: Human Rights Initiatives and the Need for Alternatives to Refugee Interdiction', 26 *Cornell International Law Journal* 753 (1993).
80. Guy S. Goodwin-Gill, 'Editorial: Refugees and Security', 11(1) *International Journal of Refugee Law* 1 (1999).
81. Howard Adelman, 'The Ethics of Humanitarian Intervention: The Case of the Kurdish Refugees', 6(1) *Public Affairs Quarterly* 61 (1992).
82. James Green, 'Questioning the Peremptory Status of the Prohibition of the Use of Force', 32 *Michigan Journal of International Law* 242 (2011).
83. Jerzy Sztucki, 'The Conclusions on the International Protection of Refugees adopted by the Executive Committee of the UNHCR Programme' 1(3) *International Journal of Refugee Law* 285 (1989).
84. Louise Arimatsu, 'The Law of State Responsibility in Relation to Border Crossings: An Ignored Legal Paradigm', 89 *International Law Studies* 21 (2013).
85. Luigi Condorelli, 'The Imputability to States of Acts of International Terrorism', 19 *Israel Yearbook on Human Rights* 233 (1989).
86. Luke T. Lee, 'Toward a World without Refugees: The United Nations Group of Governmental Experts on International Co-operation to Avert New Flows of Refugees', 57 *The British Yearbook of International Law* 317 (1986).
87. Major Jeremy A. Haugh, 'Beyond R2P: A Proposed Test For Legalizing Unilateral Armed Humanitarian Intervention' 221 *Military Law Review* 1 (2014).
88. Mark R. Hutchinson, 'Restoring Hope: UN Security Council Resolutions for Somalia and an expanded doctrine of Humanitarian Intervention', 34 *Harvard International Law Journal* 624 (1993).
89. Michael N. Schmitt, 'Preemptive Strategies in International Law', 24 *Michigan Journal of International Law* 513 (2003).
90. Milena Sterio, 'Humanitarian Intervention Post-Syria: Legitimate and Legal?', 40 *Brooklyn Journal of International Law* 109 (2014).
91. Myron Weiner, 'Security, Stability, and International Migration', 17(3) *International Security* 91 (1992-3).
92. Myron Weiner & Münz Rainer, 'Migrants, refugees and foreign policy: prevention and intervention strategies', 18(1) *Third World Quarterly* 25 (1997).
93. Nicholas Tsagourias, 'Necessity and the Use of Force: A Special Regime' in I. F. Dekker and E. Hey (eds) 41 *Netherlands Yearbook of International Law* 11 (2010).
94. Oona A. Hathaway, Tomas, VIctor, Brower & Liss, 'Consent-Based Humanitarian Intervention: Giving Sovereign Responsibility Back to the Sovereign' 46 *Cornell Internaitonal Law Journal* 499 (2013).
95. Pierre Laberge, 'Humanitarian Intervention: Three Ethical Positions', 9 *Ethics and International Affairs* 15 (1995).
96. Pierre-Marie Dupuy, 'Reviewing the Difficulties of Codification: On Ago's Classification of Obligations of Means and Obligations of Result in Relation to State Responsibility', 10(2) *European Journal of International Law* 371 (1999).

97. Robert P. Barnidge, Jr. 'The Due Diligence Principle Under International Law', 8 *International Community Law Review* 81 (2006).
98. Robert Y. Jennings, 'Some International Law Aspects of the Refugee Question', 20 *British Yearbook of International Law* 98 (1939).
99. Roman Boed, 'State of Necessity as a Justification for Internationally Wrongful Conduct', 3 *Yale Human Rights and Development Law Journal* 1 (2000).
100. Ulf Linderfalk, 'The Effect of Jus Cogens Norms: Whoever Opened Pandora's Box, Did You Ever Think About the Consequences?', 18 *European Journal of International Law* 853 (2007).
101. Vaughan Lowe, 'Precluding Wrongfulness or Responsibility: A Plea for Excuses', 10 *European Journal of International Law* 405 (1999).
102. Ved P. Nanda 'The Future Under International Law of the Responsibility to Protect after Libya and Syria', 21(1) *Michigan State International Law Review* 1 (2013).

Conference Papers and Reports

103. International Law Association, Draft Report on Aggression and the Use of Force (Johannesburg Conference, May 2016).
104. International Law Association, Final Report on the Meaning of Armed Conflict in International Law (The Hague Conference, 2010).
105. Wolff Heintschel von Heinegg, 'Legal Implications of Territorial Sovereignty in Cyberspace', in: C. Czosseck, R. Ottis & K. Ziolkowski (eds), *4th International Conference on Cyber Conflict* (Tallinn: NATO CCD COE Publications, 2012) 7.

Newspaper Articles

106. Diyar Guldogan, 'Syrian operation is to clear Daesh, says Turkish FM' *Anadolu Agency*, 24 August 2016, available at: http://aa.com.tr/en/politics/syrian-operation-is-to-clear-daesh-says-turkish-fm-/634440 [accessed: 5 September 2016].
107. Euan McKirdy, Jason Hanna & Isil Sariyuce, 'Turkey sends tanks into Syria against ISIS; rebels reportedly capture town' *CNN*, 24 August 2016, (Available at: http://edition.cnn.com/2016/08/24/middleeast/turkish-troops-isis-syria-operation/index.html [accessed: 4 September 2016].
108. Humeyra Pamuk & Seda Sezer, 'At G20 meeting, Turkey pushes plan for "safe zone" in Syria', *Reuters*, 5 September 2016, available at: http://in.reuters.com/article/g20-turkey-syria-idINKCN11B1FF [accessed: 9 September 2016].
109. Kılıç Bugra Kanat, 'DAESH and PKK attack Turkey again', *Daily Sabah*, 21 August 2016, available at: http://www.dailysabah.com/columns/kilic-bugra-kanat/2016/08/21/daesh-and-pkk-attack-turkey-again [accessed: 21 August 2016].
110. Lizzie Dearden, 'Russia and Syria 'weaponising' refugee crisis to destabilise Europe, Nato commander claims', *Independent*, 3 March 2016, available at: http://www.independent.co.uk/news/world/middle-east/russia-and-syria-weaponising-refugee-crisis-to-destabilise-europe-nato-commander-claims-a6909241.html [accessed: 12 July 2016].
111. Louis Charbonneau & Michelle Nichols, 'U.N. Security Council Powers Meet Again on Syria; No Outcome', *Reuters*, 29 August 2013, available at: http://www.reuters.com/article/2013/08/29/us-syria-crisis-un-idUSBRE97S17R20130829 [accessed: 5 July 2016].
112. Mark Lowen, 'Syria conflict: Life returns to Jarablus after IS flees' *BBC News*, 13 September 2016, available at: http://www.bbc.com/news/world-middle-east-37350970 [accessed: 13 September 2016].

113. Mehmet Cetingulec, 'How long can Turkey afford growing refugee bill?', *Al Monitor*, 26 April 2016, available at: http://www.al-monitor.com/pulse/originals/2016/05/turkey-syria-growing-refugee-bill.html, [accessed: 12 July 2016].
114. Murat Sofuoglu, "Safe zone' calls for Syrian refugees in an unsafe country', *TRTWORLD*, 25 April 2016 available at: http://www.trtworld.com/in-depth/safe-zone-calls-for-syrian-refugees-in-an-unsafe-country-93759 [accessed: 5 September 2016].
115. Tim Arango, Anne Barnard & Ceylan Yeginsu, 'Turkish-backed rebels drive IS from Syrian town Jarablus' *The Globe and Mail Online*, 24 August 2016, available at: http://www.theglobeandmail.com/news/world/turkey-starts-targeted-operations-against-islamic-state-syrian-fighters/article31528917/ [accessed 4 September 2016].
116. 'FSA launches new phase to liberate Syria's Al-Bab', *Anadolu Agency*, 13 November 2016, available at: http://aa.com.tr/en/info/infographic/2504 [accessed: 13 November 2016].
117. 'Security corridor in Azaz-Jarabulus expands', *Anadolu Agency*, 6 September 2016, available at: http://aa.com.tr/en/info/infographic/1888 [accessed: 10 September 2016].
118. 'Terrorist PKK, PYD are 'exactly same thing,' says Barzani', *TRTWORLD*, 23 March 2016, available at: http://www.trtworld.com/mea/terrorist-pkk-pyd-are-exactly-same-thing-says-barzani-73972 [accessed: 12 July 2016].
119. 'Turkish army in Syria in response to continuous terrorist attacks, President Erdogan says' *Daily Sabah*, 24 August 2016, available at: http://www.dailysabah.com/war-on-terror/2016/08/24/turkish-army-in-syria-in-response-to-continuous-terrorist-attacks-president-erdogan-says [accessed: 4 September 2016].
120. 'Turkish border with Syria cleared of Daesh terrorists', *Anadolu Agency*, 4 September 2016, available at: http://aa.com.tr/en/info/infographic/1871 [accessed: 10 September 2016].

Other Sources

121. David Kaye, 'Harold Koh's Case for Humanitarian Intervention', *Just Security*, 7 October 2013, available at: https://www.justsecurity.org/1730/kaye-kohs-case/ [accessed: 12 July 2016].
122. European Commission Humanitarian Aid and Civil Protection, *Turkey: Refugee Crisis*, September 2016, at 1, available at: http://ec.europa.eu/echo/files/aid/countries/factsheets/turkey_syrian_crisis_en.pdf [accessed: 9 September 2016].
123. Harold Hongju Koh, 'Another Legal View of the Dissent Channel Cable on Syria' *Just Security*, 20 June 2016, available at: https://www.justsecurity.org/31571/legal-view-dissent-channel-cable-syria/ [accessed: 4 September 2016].
124. Harold Hongju Koh, 'Syria and the Law of Humanitarian Intervention (Part I: Political Miscues and U.S. Law)' *Just Security*, 26 September 2013, available at: https://www.justsecurity.org/1158/koh-syria/ [accessed: 12 July 2016].
125. Harold Hongju Koh, 'Syria and the Law of Humanitarian Intervention (Part II: International Law and the Way Forward)' *Just Security*, 2 October 2013, available at: https://www.justsecurity.org/1506/koh-syria-part2/: [accessed: 12 July 2016].
126. Harold Hongju Koh, 'Syria and the Law of Humanitarian Intervention (Part III – A Reply)' *Just Security*, 10 October 2013, available at: https://www.justsecurity.org/1863/syria-law-humanitarian-intervention-part-iii-reply/ [accessed: 12 July 2016].
127. Internal Displacement Monitoring Centre (IDMC) of the Norwegian Refugee Council, 'Syria IDP Figures Analysis', available at: http://www.internal-displacement.org/middle-east-and-north-africa/syria/figures-analysis [accessed: 14 September 2016].
128. Jihad Yazigi, 'No Going Back: Why Decentralisation is the Future for Syria', European Council On Foreign Relations, September 2016, at 5, available at: http://www.ecfr.eu/page/-/ECFR185_-_NO_GOING_BACK_-_WHY_DECENTRALISATION_IS_THE_FUTURE_FOR_SYRIA.pdf [accessed: 9 September 2016].

129. Migration Policy Centre, *Registered Syrian refugees by country of asylum*, (data taken from Eurostat [EU28, Norway and Switzerland]; UNHCR [Turkey, Lebanon, Jordan, Iraq and Egypt]) available at: http://www.migrationpolicycentre.eu/migrant-crisis/focus-on-syrians/ [accessed: 4 September 2016].
130. Oytun Orhan & Sabiha Senyücel Gundogar, *Effects of the Syrian Refugees on Turkey*, January 2015, ORSAM Report No: 195, available at: http://www.orsam.org.tr/files/Raporlar/rapor195/195eng.pdf [accessed: 12 July 2016].
131. Republic of Turkey Ministry of Interior Directorate General of Migration Management, *Temporary Protection*, available at: http://www.goc.gov.tr/icerik3/temporary-protection_915_1024_4748 [accessed: 14 November 2016].
132. Syrian Observatory for Human Rights, 'About 430 thousands were killed since the beginning of the Syrian revolution' 13 September 2016, available at: http://www.syriahr.com/en/?p=50612 [accessed: 14 September 2016].
133. The World Bank Group, Overview per country, available at: http://data.worldbank.org/indicator/SP.POP.TOTL [accessed: 4 September 2016].
134. Wolff Heintschel von Heinegg, Lecture on 20 November 2015: Current Issues of the Law of Armed Conflict, Frankfurt (Oder), European University Viadrina.
135. 'Speakers Call for Voluntary Suspension of Veto Rights in Cases of Mass Atrocity Crimes, as Security Council Debates Working Methods', *Security Council 7052nd Meeting*, 29 October 2013, available at: http://www.un.org/press/en/2013/sc11164.doc.htm [accessed: 12 July 2016].

List of Cases

Air Service Agreement of 27 March 1946 (US v France), 18 RIAA 416 *(1978).*

Barcelona Traction, Light and Power Company, Limited (Belgium v Spain), Second Phase, Judgment, ICJ Reports 1970, 3.

CMS Gas Transmission Company v Argentine Republic, 14 ICSID Reports 152 (2005).

Corfu Channel (United Kingdom v Albania), ICJ Reports 1949, 1.

Forests of Central Rhodope (Greece v Bulgaria), 3 UNRIAA 1405 (1933).

Gabčíkovo-Nagymaros Project (Hungary v Slovakia), ICJ Reports 1997, 7.

LaGrand (Germany v USA), ICJ Reports 2001, 466.

Legal Consequences of the Construction of a Wall in the Occupied Palestinian Territory, Advisory Opinion, ICJ Reports 2004, 136.

Legality of Use of Force (Serbia and Montenegro v Belgium), Oral Pleading of Mr Ergec for Belgium, 10 May 1999, CR 99/15.

Military and Paramilitary Activities in and against Nicaragua (Nicaragua v US), ICJ Reports 1986, 14.

Naulilaa Incident (Portugal v Germany) 2 RIAA 1011 (1928).

Oil Platforms (US v Iran), ICJ Reports 2003, 1.

Oil Platforms (US v Iran), ICJ Reports 2003, 1, at 324-361 (Judge Simma, sep op).

Properties of the Bulgarian Minorities in Greece, II(2) ILC Yearbook 34 (1980).

Prosecutor v Mucić *et al,* Case No. IT-96-21-T, Judgement (Trial Chamber), para 184 (ICTY, 16 November 1998).

Prosecutor v Tadić, Case, No IT-94-1, Decision on Defence Motion for Interlocutory Appeal on Jurisdiction, para 70 (ICTY, 2 October 1995).

Rainbow Warrior (New Zealand v France) 20 RIAA 215 (1990).

Rights of Nationals of the United States of America in Morocco (France v US), ICJ Reports 1952, 176.

Trail Smelter Arbitration (United States v Canada), 35 American Journal of International Law 684 (1941).

L.B. Çetinkaya, *Safe Zone*, SpringerBriefs in Law,
DOI 10.1007/978-3-319-51997-5

Kolibri 360 GmbH
Ferdinand-Jühlke-Straße 7
99095 Erfurt, Deutschland
produktsicherheit@kolibri360.de